Best Wishes

Mark Hamill

Diamond
Quality
Leadership

Diamond Quality Leadership

The Six Qualities that Separate the Best Leaders from the Rest

Mark Hinderliter

iUniverse, Inc.
New York Lincoln Shanghai

Diamond Quality Leadership
The Six Qualities that Separate the Best Leaders from the Rest

iUniverse books may be ordered through booksellers or by contacting:

iUniverse
2021 Pine Lake Road, Suite 100
Lincoln, NE 68512
www.iuniverse.com
1-800-Authors (1-800-288-4677)

Because of the dynamic nature of the Internet, any Web addresses or links contained in this book may have changed since publication and may no longer be valid.

The views expressed in this work are solely those of the author and do not necessarily reflect the views of the publisher, and the publisher hereby disclaims any responsibility for them.

"Tackle Your Toughest Challenge Today", from FIERCE CONVERSATIONS by Susan Scott, copyright(c) 2002 by Fierce Conversations, Inc. Used by permission of Viking Penguin, a division of Penguin Group (USA) Inc.

ISBN: 978-0-595-44046-7 (pbk)
ISBN: 978-0-595-69356-6 (cloth))
ISBN: 978-0-595-88369-1 (ebk)

Printed in the United States of America

To my wife Sandy, the love of my life.

To my sons, Charlie, Andrew, and Jonathan—three young men of great character.

Contents

Acknowledgments

There are so many to thank for their inspiration and guidance on this book. I am indebted to so many generous people.

It starts with my guests on the radio show who shared their insights and practical knowledge of leadership. They inspired the leadership model that inspired the book.

I am deeply grateful to Bud Cummings of Professional Development Associates in Abilene, Texas. Bud is one of my greatest mentors in this business. He's taught me so many things, and gave me the idea of asking my radio guests about what differentiates great leadership from good leadership.

Mel Nelson is a friend from Fargo, North Dakota, who offers me weekly encouragement, wisdom, and prayer.

Interestingly, I have three other mentors whom I have never met who have influenced my work. They are Gus Lee, author of *Courage, the Backbone of Leadership*, Dr. Relly Nadler, author of *Leader's Playbook*, and Susan Scott, author of *Fierce Conversations*. Gus Lee gave me deeper insight into courage and its role in leadership. I learned the concept of micro-initiatives from Relly Nadler. I learned how to improve at having deep, meaningful dialogue at home and work from Susan Scott. They've taught me through sharing their insights on my radio show and in their writings, which I have used as resources for my workshops and this book. I highly recommend their books.

I am indebted to several people who read the manuscript, gave me feedback, and made the book better. They are Judy West, Gina Birkemeier, Linda Monday, Barbara Parker, Steve Glickman, and Sandy Hinderliter.

I am grateful to all the people I've worked with over the years that have taught me so much and inspired many of the stories I've used to try to illustrate my teaching points.

I am grateful to Brad and Kathy Lambert, co-executive directors of Connections to Success, for allowing Sandy and me the opportunity to work with the men and women in their faith-based program and to help them reenter the community from the corrections system. A special thanks to Bill and others in the program for showing us what it really takes to change and grow in the face of obstacles.

I am without the words to express my love and gratitude for Sandy Hinderliter, my wife, soul mate, greatest friend, and ally.

What would genuine gratitude be without giving thanks to a loving God who keeps blessing me by putting extraordinary people in my path?

Preface

While I have been working in leadership development for over twenty years, I have gained a much deeper insight into the change and growth process working in another arena. It's funny where life's lessons can come from if we are open to them. My wife, Sandy, and I have worked with men and women returning to the community from the prison system. We worked with a faith-based organization that offered a holistic program to ex-offenders that included training, mentoring, and other types of support, such as help in finding housing, transportation, and employment.

The odds against ex-felons are daunting. Statistics I've seen indicate that two out of three people who have been in prison eventually go back. The faith-based initiative we worked with and others like it work to change those outcomes. After working with over a hundred men, I saw some of them make significant changes in their lives and become productive citizens, and others not make the needed changes and end up going back to prison. While the outcomes in this program were dramatically better than the national norms, a question kept coming back to me: *Why did some of the men and women make the changes needed to successfully reenter the community, where others did not?* What we discovered was it wasn't any one factor that made the difference; it was always a combination of things the successful people did that created change in the face of tremendous odds. The best way I know how to describe them is to tell the story of one of the men we worked with. His name has been changed.

Bill's story

Sandy and I have worked with Bill for about three years. He is in his mid-fifties. Bill spent most of his adult life in federal prison.

He grew up in a tough neighborhood on the south side of Chicago in an abusive home. In his late teens he was convicted of kidnapping and spent sixteen years in federal prisons. After being released and placed on probation, he went back to his old ways.

Over the next couple of decades, Bill's probation was revoked, and he was sent back to prison eight to ten times (he can't remember the exact number) for repeat offenses. Bill was the definition of a career criminal. His criminal ways continued in prison. While in prison, he was the guy who "ran things." If an inmate wanted something, he usually had to go through Bill. By his own admission, he was a *bad guy*. Because of the influence he was able to exert, he was often transferred to other federal facilities around the country.

A few years ago, after his latest release from prison, Bill was told by his federal probation officer to participate in a program that included training and follow-up support to help him succeed—or go back to prison. That is how we met Bill. My role in the program was to conduct what is called "reentry training." It was an eight-day class designed to help men make the transition to reentering the community. Bill was like many of the men in the program—angry and cynical.

Somewhere along the line, Bill started to open up and a breakthrough occurred. I asked him many months later, while doing some follow-up mentoring, "Bill, what is different now? You have been revoked at least eight times, and now you're doing all the right things to get it together. Why?" He told me very simply he had decided to change. He said it was his responsibility and no one else's. He knew that he would go back to prison for life without that fundamental commitment.

Over time, one thing became pretty clear to me about Bill. He was committed to change. He was motivated. But, he had no idea how to change or what to change to. Functioning in a community, in a family, and in a workplace was new territory to him. What he knew was how to operate on the street or in a prison. He knew that those models would not work any longer but did not know what a new model for living might be. Having great survival skills and powers of observation, he instinctively knew he needed new models, so he started hanging out at the faith-based agency and watching for people he could emulate. He found a couple and stuck to them like glue.

One of the next things Bill had to do once he had been out of prison for a while was to assess what was and was not working for him. That was a pretty complex job that required help. In the training I conducted, and in the follow-up work with him, Sandy and I had to engage him in many conversations examining his patterns of thoughts and behaviors and how they were helping or hurting his cause. Coping skills that helped him in the prison system could very well hold him back in this new world. We also had to help him examine his employment-related skills. Research indicated that unemployment was the number one predictor of recidivism. Some 80 percent of those who go back to prison are unemployed.

Assessing what was and was not working for Bill helped us identify some necessary changes. Reinventing ourselves is difficult to do. What all of us can do is make small but critical changes that have major impact. Bill made three very doable changes. He joined AA; he started spending time with different, healthier people; and he focused on landing and keeping a job. The results have been remarkable. The first two changes enabled Bill to accomplish the third—land and keep a good job. For the first time in his life, Bill has a real job with benefits. He knew that the number one factor that keeps people from going back to prison is maintaining employment. Those targeted changes made all the difference.

One of the sad experiences of working with men who have been in the prison system comes when I ask them, "Who is in your life that will support you in achieving your goals?" Typically, three out of four tell me "no one." That may be the biggest obstacle to sustaining success. Bill knew instinctively that he needed a few people to help keep him going forward. He needed mentors. I became one of those mentors. One thing is perfectly clear to me—Bill could have followed the first steps faithfully and would have utterly failed without the support of mentors. I would extend that comment to virtually all the participants we have worked with. There have been too many bumps in the road that would have derailed him left on his own. There have also been many situations he has encountered that were new to him, where he needed coaching and guidance.

About a year into the program, Bill called and asked me to take him to a drug and alcohol treatment program. It was a two-hour drive to the facility, so we had a chance to talk. He admitted he had been "using" again and had a heart-to-heart talk with his probation officer, and they agreed that checking into this thirty-day treatment program was the best course of action. What was interesting to me was that Bill was beginning to step up when it really mattered, possibly for the first time. I saw three indications of that. First, he was being honest with himself and others about what he was doing. Second, he was recommitting to doing things the right way. Third, he was deciding to keep the commitment he had made to himself, and others, to making serious change. This was a breakthrough moment. Bill chose to step up when it mattered most.

Bill faced many bumps in the road to transform from a career criminal to a productive citizen. What was amazing about Bill was that he faced them and kept going forward. He refused to quit. That dogged persistence has served him well because his journey forward has been one challenge after another.

So, why share Bill's story in a book about leadership? The epiphany for me in working with Bill and others was that the keys to Bill's change and growth are the same keys to the growth process for leaders. Leadership development is about change and growth. The circumstances are certainly different, the objectives and obstacles are different, but the process of change and growth in the leadership arena include many of the same things that helped Bill breakthrough.

I consider them to be the seven keys to creating breakthroughs.

1. Commit to change and personal growth.
2. Find and follow a success model.
3. Assess what is and isn't working.

4. Implement small strategic changes that will make the most difference.

5. Engage ongoing support through a coach or mentors.

6. Step up when it matters most.

7. Persist in the face of all obstacles.

Bill, unlike many of the others, was very intentional about succeeding. I've found that leaders committed to their growth are similarly intentional. They don't leave success to chance. Their intentionality and persistence, like Bill's, set them apart from the pack.

Introduction

I've worked in the leadership development arena for about twenty years and have worked with managers at all levels all over the world. I've worked in multiple business sectors including retail, sales, IT, software development, health care, manufacturing, higher education and non-profit. What is striking to me is that most managers and leaders struggle with the same issues; challenges with leading people, managing change, too little time and too few resources, and working too many hours at the expense of their own well-being.

Instead of another dry textbook approach to leadership development, I chose to write a story about a manager who has the same struggles as many of my clients. My sense is that readers could relate to his story because in many ways, it is their story. The manager's name is Denny Collins. He is a composite of so many people I have met in my work. Denny is a regional manager for a (fictional) retail chain, and in spite of a tremendous work ethic, his performance as a manager has been disappointing to his boss and himself.

To get back to the performance level he once achieved, Denny keeps working more and more hours. Unfortunately, working more is *not* improving his effectiveness or performance. It's only alienating his family and risking personal burnout.

Denny works his way through these challenges with the help of an executive coach—Coach Kay. Kay shares with Denny a leadership model that differentiates great leaders from good ones, and how to implement it in practical and meaningful ways.

My encouragement to you is to enjoy the story and see how it relates to your life, and if the leadership model and any of the solutions Denny and Kay discover work for you.

At the end of the story I discuss the leadership model Kay uses with Denny. It is the *Diamond Leadership Model©* that I discovered conducting in-depth interviews with high-level executives over a two-year period. Included in that overview are practical tips and tools you can use to implement this model in your own leadership role. My clients have used these tips and tools with much success.

Best wishes.

Mark Hinderliter
President, The AbeL Group, LLC
St Louis, MO

Chapter 1

Reflections

Life is just a mirror, and what you see out there, you must first see inside of you.

Wally "Famous" Amos

My name is Denny Collins. I am a regional manager for a company called The Cooking Store. We have a chain of stores that sell upscale kitchen equipment and conduct cooking classes for men and women of all ages. In our stores, we have every appliance and gadget a novice or professional cook could want. We also have a professional kitchen with stadium seating to accommodate cooking-class participants. It's a pretty cool set-up and business. It even smells good.

I am a husband and father of three. I am forty-one years old and have the body of a man who enjoys cooking, if you know what I mean. I am not the Goodyear Blimp, but I am a little husky. I'd like to be in better shape, but given the choice of going to the gym to workout or making one of my homemade gourmet pizzas, the pizza wins every time. Susan is my wife of fifteen years, and we have two boys and a girl. Ronnie is thirteen, Kevin is twelve, and Julie is nine. I work hard and am a good provider for my family. I make a low six-figure income. That may not seem extraordinary, but from the very meager beginnings of my growing up, raised by a hardworking single mom who did her very best to barely scratch out a living, I guess I've come a long way. My friends I grew up with consider me a success story. Nothing was ever given to me. I joined the army after high school so I could go to college on the GI Bill. I then worked my way through college. I have a nice family and good paying professional job that I am well suited for.

Growing up with my Mom working a lot, I had to learn to cook and came to really enjoy it. I consider myself a fairly accomplished cook, so working for The Cooking Store seemed a great fit for me. I enjoy the products and services we provide. I worked my way up the ranks. Now I am in a leadership role and oversee the operations of forty stores, which are organized into six districts. Although I don't get involved as much in the day-to-day goings-on in a store, I still enjoy the business. I enjoy being in a leadership role. Growing up as I did, I guess I had to learn to take charge.

My love of cooking also allows me to enjoy a friendly rivalry with the woman I semi-affectionately call "The Mother-in-Law." At family gatherings, we have "cook-offs" and talk more smack than you'd hear at an NBA game. It adds a lot of spice to our gatherings. We both always declare victory with our dishes. The real winners of our competitions are the family members who enjoy the fare.

This year, the day after Christmas, we rented a van and drove from our St. Louis home to Florida. The van was loaded with Susan, the kids, me, The Mother-in-Law, and enough luggage and electronics to sail around the world. It was a pretty good resemblance of the Griswolds from the movie *Vacation*, without the dead aunt on the luggage rack.

We rented a condo on the beach for a week for some much-needed downtime. I probably value going on a vacation more than most people because we never went on one when I was a kid. That is, unless you count driving two hours to Springfield, Illinois, touring Abe Lincoln's home and tomb, and going to Ponderosa for dinner.

It is the morning of December 28, and I am out on the balcony drinking coffee and awaiting the 7:18 sunrise. The sunrise is close and is brightening the horizon more by the minute. Everyone else is asleep. It was a fabulous setting for reflection. The business year was coming to a close, and it was not a great year for my region.

It was a source of great frustration for me because I was accustomed to high levels of performance. Because I grew up with very little, I've always been driven to achieve as much as I could. I am blessed with a great work ethic that I give my mother credit for. She had very little education and had to work at low-paying jobs as a result. But she did work hard, often with two jobs to help us make ends meet. Working as hard as she did and raising my brother and me took its toll. Combined with her one and only vice, smoking, her body just gave out. May God rest her soul. I owe her so much for the sacrifices she made, but I admit to still feeling some anger at her for the years of smoking that took her too early. I am grateful that Susan and I were able to give her some nice things and take her on a few vacations like this one. If any of my children take up smoking, they will be fortunate that they won't experience lung cancer or heart disease from it. Not because of medical advances, but because I will kill them myself.

My mother's work ethic has served me well, but now it feels like no matter what I do, it's never enough. I could literally spend twenty-four hours a day, seven days a week working and not get it all done. For the first time in my career, my performance was suffering and working harder wasn't helping. The only thing working more seemed to be accomplishing was wearing me out and distancing me from my family. Work and family life are now pretty much conducted on the dead run from one meeting to the next, from one of the kids' events to the next. To quote George Jetson, "Jane, stop this crazy thing."

The sunrise broke onto the horizon and grabbed me and pulled me out of my thoughts. It was spectacular as it burned orange and brought light to a new day. It reminded me of how extraordinary God's creation is and that we were not meant for a shallow, mediocre existence—and that each sunrise brought with it new possibilities.

Our pastor often says that we are created to be in a relationship with our maker and with each other. I think he is right about that. It's our important relationships that matter, and this hustle-bustle existence seems to be the enemy of deep, meaningful relationships.

My family is what matters most to me. And, I have a few friends that I would do anything for. As I think about it, that's where the joy of my role as a regional manager comes from—working with quality people and helping them grow and prosper. In the business I am in, the competitive advantage we have is quality people. Our competitors have similar products, comparable technology, and locations that are, for the most part, placed in the marketplace as well as ours are.

My solitude was broken when Julie, our nine-year-old daughter, sleepily came out on the balcony and curled up on my lap. We watched the rest of the sunrise together, and I became quietly emotional. It was a perfect moment.

The rest of the vacation was enjoyable, like the moment with Julie and some football on the beach with the boys, yet also a little disconcerting. Many of my thoughts the rest of the week were about how it felt like I was failing on the business and the home fronts.

As I was holding Julie, she reminded me so much of her mother. Susan has been nothing short of a godsend for me. We met on a blind date that I didn't want to go on, but a mutual friend of ours wouldn't take no for an answer. Life is funny like that, because after four dates, I knew I had met my soul mate. I proposed at a St. Louis Cardinals baseball game—with nacho cheese spilled down my shirt. We were married six months later. She has been my true love and my Rock of Gibraltar. She is also a wonderful mother.

Lately, I have this nagging feeling that I am failing her. Because I have been putting in so many hours to get back to a high level of performance, I find myself giving her very little time and attention. She is a sweet and gentle soul and never complains, but I can see the pain in her eyes and on her face. I felt a surge of new commitment to work on my marriage. I had a sense that getting my work life in order was the key to freeing me up to invest the time necessary to get my family life in order. As far as a starting point, I felt as lost as a month-old Easter egg.

Chapter 2

Testing the Open Door

Trust men and they will be true to you; treat them greatly, and they will show themselves great.

Ralph Waldo Emerson

Vacation, as always, went too fast. After more soul searching, it became clear to me that it was important for me to work in such a way that I could be even more effective than I am now but also create more balance in my life to be a better husband, father, and friend. The work and family priorities are in reverse order, but I felt strongly that improved effectiveness in my job was the key to becoming more available to my family.

My boss is Steve Gillman, director of operations of the company. I called him after vacation and set up a meeting to talk about my concerns. He's not the kind of leader who says he has an open door but fails to warn you that there is a pit bull inside waiting to bite your face off if you aren't careful. We generally shoot straight with each other. I really respect that about him. Nevertheless, I felt some anxiety about telling my boss I was working too hard. After some small talk, I got right to it.

"Steve, I know my region underperformed this year and there are improvements we need to make. I have been busting my butt to get the region back to where it needs to be, and I don't seem to be making progress. I thought that working harder would solve the problem, and it hasn't. All it seems to do is distance me from my family, and I am feeling pretty lousy about it." This was not a conversation I would have unless I really trusted my boss.

Steve thought for a second before he replied. "I can see this is really important to you, and knowing you as I do, you've given it a lot of thought. Tell me more." I admired how he made it safe to talk about sensitive stuff. I am not sure I always do that for my direct reports.

"You know my work ethic. I put in fifty to sixty hours a week and even more during the holiday seasons. Lately, it just seems like I can never get it all done. I truly believe that even if I worked 24/7, there would still be more to do." I could hear myself sounding a little whiney. I hate complaining. Steve just kept listening, so I continued. "It is really important to me to achieve excellence in my region, but how much more can I give? It's now to the point where it's affecting my family life." A wave of emotion gripped me, and I couldn't say any more. I sat there feeling embarrassed.

"So, you're feeling that your commitment to excellence in your job is compromising that same commitment you have to your family. And because both are really important to you, you are really troubled. Is that what I am hearing?" Steve reflected. All I could do was nod in agreement as I continued to battle my emotions.

Steve paused for another moment; I think to give me time to gather myself. I admire his patience. Finally, I blurted out, "Look, I'm sorry I am so emotional."

"Denny," Steve responded firmly, "you don't need to apologize for being passionate about your family and career. In fact, it's what I admire most about you—that you care so deeply and are so committed."

"Thanks. That means a lot to me. Do you have any words of wisdom? You've probably been in my shoes. You're successful and have a family. Surely you have some feedback," I said hopefully.

"Before I offer my thoughts, I know you've given this some thought. Any possible solutions on your mind?"

I jumped on the question. "Absolutely. Reduce my workweek to forty-five to fifty hours while improving performance and spend more time with my family. You know, like *Mission Impossible*."

"Any thoughts on how to accomplish that?"

"Steve, if I knew that, I wouldn't be in here crying like a teenage girl," I laughed.

He smiled and then waited. I could see that I wasn't going to get off that easily. So, I continued, "I don't think there is a silver bullet. I could probably manage my time a little more effectively, possibly stay more focused and delegate a little more. That's what I've been kicking around anyway. As far as any details behind any of those things, I haven't figured that out yet. What do you think, Steve?" I was really interested in his feedback.

He thought for a moment. "It sounds to me like you're generally on the right track. I don't have a good handle on how you manage your time. Because of our travel schedules, we don't see each other enough for me to give you meaningful feedback. You are a pretty focused guy but could possibly benefit from a little more. My main observation is that you try to do too much yourself. My sense is that you could develop your people more through delegating and coaching. They would benefit as well."

We sat there for a moment while his feedback sunk in. I thought I was pretty good at developing people but was open to his feedback. I sat there wondering how to turn those general ideas into something specific I could execute. I am all about execution.

"Let me toss an idea out," Steve offered, as if he was reading my mind. "You are a really valuable person to this organization. You're passionate about what you do and do an excellent job. I worked with a coach in my previous company and really benefited from an objective professional helping me look at my strengths and developmental issues. She helped me deal with current challenges and take my leadership skills and performance to another level. She also helped me with the balance issue. If you're game, I'd be willing to make the investment in coaching to help you work through this challenge."

I felt a surge of hope and gladly accepted. Steve said he would contact the coach and that she would give me a call.

Before we left, Steve set a follow-up appointment for us to see how it was going. I walked out of his office with a deep resolve to get on top of this. This conversation was a reminder to me why I feel such a deep loyalty to Steve. While it seems to me that loyalty is eroding in corporate America, I am still convinced that people are loyal to people. When people are valued and treated with respect, as Steve does with me and the rest of his team, loyalty and commitment is usually returned. Personally, I'd run through a brick wall for the guy if he asked me to.

Chapter 3

Coach Kay

The best teacher is the one who suggests rather than dogmatizes, and inspires his listener with the wish to teach himself.

Edward Bulwer-Lytton

A couple of days after my meeting with Steve, I received an e-mail from Kay Michaels, executive coach. At least, that's what was on her signature line. The e-mail was to introduce her and let me know that this was a follow-up to the call she received from Steve. After trading a couple of e-mails, we settled on a date for our first coaching session. I found myself eagerly anticipating it.

The coaching would all be conducted on the telephone, and the first session was pretty much a "getting to know each other" session. She shared her background and asked me a lot of questions about my background, my personal and professional goals, key successes, and current challenges. I shared the concerns that I shared with Steve. I told her that my primary objectives were to improve my performance in my regional manager role and to somehow work smarter so I could spend more time with my family. After some more conversation, I asked, "Coach Kay, how is this coaching going to work?" Kay laughed that I called her Coach Kay, so I had to explain that my wife is a college basketball fan, and that Duke is her team, led by Mike Krzyzewski, or the legendary Coach K.

"The question about the coaching process is a great question" she noted. "Typically, it works like this. After getting to know each other and getting clear about your objectives, I will lay some foundation for the work we will do. First, I like to share a leadership model that my research shows differentiates great leaders from good ones. Then, I'd like to work with you to conduct a 360 feedback assessment based on that leadership model. That will give us a great starting point to understand what you are doing well and what you might improve. After that, we'll work together to identify what to work on and then go to work. Then, after several months, we might want to do a follow-up 360 feedback assessment to measure your progress and where to go from there." She paused and asked, "What are your thoughts, Denny, about what I've described?"

"Sounds pretty intense."

She laughed. "I don't know if intense is the right word, but it is a commitment." She turned serious. "Given what you've described to me about feeling overburdened, is that a commitment you want to take on?"

Pause. "Yes."

"I am glad to hear that," she replied. "In our next session, I'll lay some groundwork by sharing a leadership model that I find helps leaders go to the next level in their effectiveness. What questions or comments do you have?"

"It still sounds pretty intense."

Chapter 4

Diamond Quality Leadership

Great leadership is the only sustainable competitive advantage. Every thing else can be copied.

Dr. Gerald Bell

The next couple of weeks were very hectic. There was no slowdown from the Christmas holiday season. At the beginning of the year, there are new products to get into the stores, product training to conduct, goal setting sessions with my direct reports, and new marketing efforts to kick off the year. So, as usual, I had to put in a lot of hours, and again it was the family that suffered from my lack of presence. I was looking forward to the coaching because I was still stuck in the same pattern. I'm a little ashamed to say this, but I hadn't yet shared with Susan that I had a coach. I was afraid that I would create some expectations that I couldn't fulfill.

The next coaching session began with the usual check-in process to see how it was going. Then, Coach Kay began her explanation of what she called the "Diamond Leadership Model."

"Denny," Kay began, "in my role as a leadership coach, I have worked with hundreds of executives from all kinds of industries, including government leaders. I've always been curious about what differentiates great leadership from good leadership, so I ask all my clients, 'what, in your experience, have you seen that differentiates great leaders from good ones?'

"It always results in a fascinating conversation. My clients are people running organizations, divisions, regions, and departments where their leadership is on the line everyday. They are the voices of experience. After asking them that question for several years, something interesting happened—some themes emerged from that question and their answers. Six clear themes bubbled up as to what the leadership differentiators were. So, I have created what I call the Diamond Leadership Model based on what makes leaders a cut above.

"Before I share the model with you, I'd like to get your response to the question about what differentiates great from good leadership. What do you think?" she asked me.

"Well," I said to buy some time to think. "I definitely think character plays a role. Probably vision. I would probably add charisma. Great leaders seem to have magnetic personalities." I was satisfied with my answer. "I guess that's it. What have you discovered?"

"I'd like you to draw a five-point diamond on a piece of paper."

I drew the diamond. Kay told me to title it the Diamond Leadership Model and began to share with me the six differentiators and where to put them on the diamond.

"My experience shows that it can be really helpful to have a mental model of a concept that you want to get hold of," she explained.

The Diamond Leadership Model

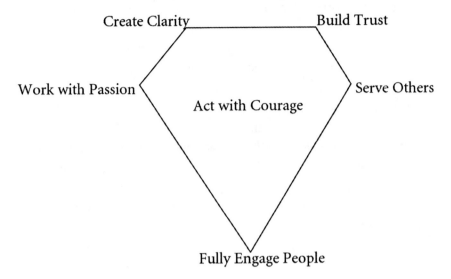

Create Clarity · Build Trust · Work with Passion · Act with Courage · Serve Others · Fully Engage People

She continued, "Let me flush these ideas out a little more by making these terms more descriptive and adding a few quotes from some of my clients that should add meaning.

"The first is 'create clarity.' I bet you'll agree, Denny, in a world of unrelenting time pressures, fierce competition, and constant change, clarity is critical. A couple of quotes from my clients illustrate."

We totally changed our culture and level of performance when we implemented five simple principles and started living by them—Pick it up on time, deliver it on time, don't break it, bill it accurately, and recover quickly if we make a mistake.

*   *   *

In our organization, we have three simple rules we live by: one, we work for the customer; two, we work for the customer; and three, we work for the customer. Every associate knows it, and it empowers them to do the right thing during those moments of truth.

"What do you think, Denny? Is everyone in your region crystal clear about what the business objectives are and what their roles are?"

"That would be no," I said with way too much certainty.

"What if the answer was yes? What would be the impact of having everyone on the same page?" Kay challenged.

"Frankly, I think any business that had everyone in the organization rowing the boat in unison would blow away the competition, regardless of the industry. How to make that happen is the challenge," I added.

"I am wondering, Denny, in addition to impacting performance, could creating more clarity in your operation be a timesaver for you and the people in your region?" Kay asked a great question that was highly pertinent to my situation.

"Definitely!"

"Great. That sounds like something we'll be working on. Let's go on to the next differentiator, which is 'build trust.' At its core, Denny, would you agree with me that leadership is ultimately about trust?"

"You bet," I responded. "One of my favorite sayings about leadership is 'if a leader is leading and no one is following, then they are just taking a walk.'"

"That's a great line, Denny," Kay chuckled. "Let me add a few quotes from my clients."

Forget what organizations write on their Web sites and posters about their values. Just watch how their leaders behave.

*   *   *

Our people watch us. They don't always do what we say. But they do what we do.

*   *   *

There are no substitutes for telling the truth and keeping commitments for creating trust.

"I totally agree, Kay. In fact, it is one of the things I admire about my own boss. I trust him completely."

"What is the business benefit of that trust?" Kay inquired.

"I don't have to waste time looking over my shoulder, for one," I said. "I suppose another is I feel like I can take some intelligent risks in my business, like try new things, and not worry about having my head handed to me on a platter if an idea doesn't work out. That's a big deal to me."

"You are fortunate to have a manager like that. Not everyone does." Kay was dead right about that one. "Are you ready to move to the next differentiator?"

"Ready."

"It is 'work with passion.' My experience is that passion is contagious and that you can't fake it. When people work with passion, it rubs off. A couple of lines from clients."

> The great leaders I've seen turn what their organization does into a cause or a crusade and inspire people to want to be a part of it.

*   *   *

> The most successful managers I've seen have a passion for winning. They know that people really want to win, and they dedicate themselves to creating a series of small wins and turning them into a series of big wins.

The passion theme really resonated with me. "You know, Kay, as I think about my store managers that really ring true. The ones that are most successful absolutely love what they do. And, it rubs off on their staff. Interestingly, they are usually the ones with the best financial performance. Funny thing also, I have managers who are totally bottom-line driven. They are the ones who usually have employee retention problems and often make decisions that help their bottom line, often at the expense of the customer. Ironically, I've seen when managers have a total focus on the bottom line, it hurts the bottom line."

"That's a great insight, Denny. So, what do you think, can you teach your managers to be passionate about the business?

"Definitely not! In fact, I have been most successful when I hired for passion and enthusiasm and taught the business." I was firm in that conviction.

Kay continued the lesson. "The next differentiator often is a surprise to people. It is 'serve others.' I think a couple of my clients' quotes really nail it."

> Our most successful managers understand that they work for the people they lead—the ones taking care of our customers.

*   *   *

> Real leaders get it that it's not about them; it's about those they lead.

"What I would add to that, Denny is that servant leadership doesn't mean it's soft. It means providing people the tools, training and coaching, resources, and guidance they need to be successful. Holding people accountable is part of the process."

"That one does surprise me a little," I responded. "I don't know why it should because servant leadership is about two thousand years old." After a bit of reflection, I added, "Maybe it is a surprise because it isn't taught in business school and not always practiced in business. In fact, we've seen way too many examples of corporate executives landing in prison because of out-of-control self interest."

"True enough" Kay agreed. "As you think about your forty store managers, would you consider any of them servant leaders?"

"Well, I actually have six district managers that report directly to me. Each of the DMs has six to seven stores reporting to them. As I think about my district managers, most have the mentality that their job is to provide their managers with all the tools and resources necessary to be successful. I've never thought of them in terms of servant leaders because they have really high standards and hold their managers accountable."

"Do you have any district managers who don't operate that way?" she asked.

"Yes, I do. I have one who is what you might call a 'climber.' He is in it for his own career path and will do whatever it takes to advance his career." It bothered me that I had never thought about my managers from the perspective of serving others or serving themselves.

Kay's question was a mind-reader. "What is the impact on the business and the people in that district?"

"Interestingly enough, the guy gets good results. But the question that I have been wondering about is—at what cost? The cost of turnover itself is probably staggering. I've never really tried to calculate it. I really need to take a hard look at that situation." It occurred to me that I should have seen that situation more clearly before.

"Sounds like something you'll want to evaluate. You ready for the next one?"

"Yep."

"It is 'fully engage people.' One way to articulate this one is to say what it isn't. Engaging people isn't telling people what to do. The most leaders can hope to get from the 'telling' style is compliance. True commitment comes from fully engaging people's hearts, minds, and talents. A couple of quotes from my clients give some insight."

My ninety-year-old dad taught me my greatest leadership lesson—to be authentic and be interested in people and connect with them at a personal level.

*   *   *

As CEO, the most important thing I do that has the biggest impact on my business is listening to my customers and my associates. That's where many of our best ideas have come from.

The inevitable question came. Kay asked, "Who have you seen in your career that really had a knack for fully engaging people?"

Without hesitation, I answered, "My CEO at a previous company, Don Green."

Coach Kay was quiet, so I knew that was my invitation to elaborate. "Don was really approachable. When I was a district manager, he called me personally a few times to congratulate me on my performance. Even though I am a grown man and don't think I need a lot of strokes, I felt really great every time he did that."

"What else did Don do to engage people?"

"He had a great question he asked. Actually, it's a compliment and a question in one, now that I think about it. He would say, 'Denny, I know you're always thinking about ways to improve your business—what are you working on now?' That question really kept you on your toes. I wouldn't dare let him down by not having a good answer to his question. Sometimes, during a lull in a meeting, he'd ask, 'What are you thinking about?' Once, I said, 'Lunch.' He roared. He had a great sense of humor too."

I continued, on a bit of a roll, "You know the thing I really appreciated about Don is that he always asked our input in important matters about the operation. The things that would impact us. I didn't always agree with his decisions, but I always felt like I had a say and that it mattered."

"It sounds like Don really respected you, Denny."

"I believe he did, Kay, but I think it's more than that. I think it's that he respects and values people and really understands that most people really want to contribute and do a great job." It occurred to me that it was Don's deep belief in people that made him extraordinary.

"It sounds like Don was a great role model that way." Kay paused and let that sink in. "Denny, are you ready for the last differentiator?"

"Coach, I believe that would be 'act with courage,'" I pre-empted.

"It is. One of my favorite quotes about courage is from Winston Churchill. He said something like 'Courage is rightly esteemed the first of all human virtues that makes all other virtues possible.' I love that quote," Kay said. "My clients have provided some practical examples of courage in leadership."

> Great leaders give the credit during the good times and take the heat during the tough times. Weak leaders do it the other way around.

*   *   *

> We practice the philosophy, try stuff, fail fast, learn, and go forward. That philosophy encourages people to risk and innovate.

*   *   *

> Don't be afraid to tell people the truth. A culture of candor accelerates everything we do.

"Denny, where have you seen courage has been important to great leadership?"

"I guess the need for courage shows up all the time. When you have to look a good person in the eye and tell them they aren't meeting standards. Or when you have to let someone go who really tried but wasn't suited for the job. I suppose it takes courage to take the risks to try new things, knowing that they don't always work out. It takes courage to maintain our integrity—to do the right thing instead of the popular or expedient thing. As I hear myself talking, it does take a lot of backbone to lead." I suppose I really knew it but maybe didn't give courage the level of importance it really plays.

"I'll bet you've seen many examples in your career where a leader didn't act with courage, and it ended up having a negative consequence." Kay's statement was right on, and it invited a response.

"Sure. Probably what I've seen the most is not having the courage to speak with candor, to shoot completely straight with people. Sometimes, I've seen leaders not give the honest feedback that an individual needs to hear. Sometimes, it is not speaking up to the boss or someone higher up the food chain that needs to be challenged. I've seen those failures at all levels of organizations and have failed to shoot straight myself a time or two."

"What were the consequences?"

"I'll give you an example when I didn't shoot straight with an individual. I had a manager that was in a staff role and was a really hard worker. She met her deadlines and did quality work. But she wasn't a good manager or a team player. And, I overlooked it. The problem I was ignoring was that the morale on her team was poor, and the team didn't perform as well as it could have. They worked as a group of individuals. One of my direct reports who was not a member of that particular group had the courage to give me the feedback that I needed to hear: the team was suffering and I was ignoring the problem. So, I addressed the problem and told this manager, as best I could tell, her management style had been a growing problem for going on a year. The manager was angry with me. Her response was, "Why didn't you give me this feedback a year ago?" She was right, and I admitted my failure as her manager. It was a hard lesson for me. The manager failed to make the changes she needed to make, and her team suffered because I didn't muster up the courage to have the hard conversations I needed to have." It may be that I have to learn that lesson again with one of my district managers.

"That's been my experience, too, Denny. When I've seen leaders, myself included, fail to make the tough decision, shoot straight with people, or push back with higher-ups when necessary, the consequences have been devastating. In fact, if there is one truth I have found to be always true in organizations; it is that the health of the organization is directly related to the quality and candor of the dialogue. Healthy organizations, and families, have a culture of respect and candor in their discussions. They have deep, meaningful conversations where people are free to disagree and say their piece. Dysfunctional organizations play politics, don't talk with respect and candor, and sometimes don't talk in meaningful ways at all. I believe the courage to be candid and respect each other is at the bottom of it all." Kay paused and then moved to wrap up the session. "Any final questions or comments about the Diamond Leadership Model?"

"I love the model, Kay. The differentiators you've described make sense to me and what I've seen in my career. I'm wondering, why did you use the diamond as your metaphor?" I was really curious about it.

Kay laughed. "I'd like to say I gave it great thought. But that wasn't the case. It just kind of came to me when I was shopping and looking in the window of a jewelry store. It occurred to me that great leaders, like quality diamonds, are valuable—they have great clarity, they are authentic, and they are somewhat rare."

"I suppose you could say that there are diamond leaders and cubic zirconia leaders," I responded, rather proud of my observation.

"There certainly are."

At the end of the session, I decided I would put the Diamond Leadership Model on my desk as a reminder of what great leaders do.

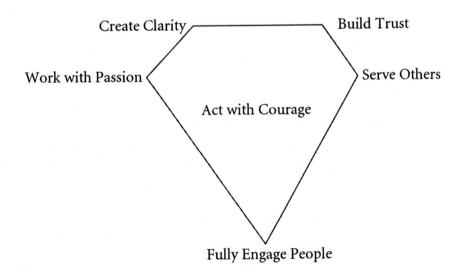

Chapter 5

Feedback

Feedback is the breakfast of champions.

Dr. Ken Blanchard

"Feedback may be the breakfast of champions, but what Ken Blanchard didn't say is it's a bran cereal breakfast. It may be good for you, but it tastes like crap," I grumped to Coach Kay at the beginning of the session after receiving the results of my 360 feedback assessment.

Coach Kay had worked with me to create and administer a 360 feedback assessment. She used an online survey tool and created a survey based on the six leadership differentiators of the Diamond Leadership Model. Each of the six became a category, and each category included five items and a couple of open-ended questions. The items were specific statements that were leadership behaviors under the six categories. I could see where the feedback would be extremely valuable in understanding my strengths and weaknesses, and how it is an important part of my development.

That is, until I read the results. The people giving feedback were my boss, a couple of peers, my six district managers, several store managers that I've worked with over the years, and the director of marketing, whom I've done some committee work with. All the surveys were anonymous.

"Tell me about your reaction to the feedback, Denny," Kay prompted.

"I work with a bunch of mental midgets. They don't get it at all. They don't get me at all." I was really perturbed.

"It sounds like you are pretty annoyed," Kay reflected.

"That's a good a good assessment," I shot back.

"OK, let's talk about it. What don't they get about you, Denny?" Kay asked patiently.

Her tone was helping me calm down a little. "Well, I don't have any specifics. I just thought the scores were pretty low, and the comments were more critical than I expected. As hard as I work, I was pretty stunned."

"What you are feeling is not unusual, Denny. Having said that, there are three common mistakes I see people make in receiving feedback. The first, and biggest, is not asking for it. You've asked, that's not an issue. The other two are getting mad at those who give the feedback and ignoring or rationalizing it."

"I understand that," I responded, "but is all feedback accurate?"

"Not necessarily. The key is to look for patterns. Should we look at the feedback together?" The coach was coaching.

For the next thirty minutes or so, Coach Kay helped me look at the data in an organized way. One way we looked at it was to review my scores on the six differentiators. This is what they were on a scale of 1–10.

Work with passion	8.89
Build trust	8.67
Act with courage	8.56
Serve others	7.34
Create clarity	6.39
Fully engage people	6.22

The second analysis we did was to look at my top five items and my bottom five items. Items were the individual statements listed under the categories. The words in bold are the categories the items fall under.

Top Five Items

1.	Works with contagious enthusiasm. (**Work with passion**)	9.35
2.	Walks the talk—demonstrates high ethical standards. (**Build trust**)	9.30
3.	Follows through on promises and commitments. (**Build trust**)	9.20
4.	Makes the tough decisions. Takes responsibility for all actions. (**Act with courage**)	9.15
5.	Pushes back (challenges decisions) from higher levels of management when appropriate. (**Act with courage**)	8.80

Bottom Five Items

1.	Communicates a clear and compelling vision of where the business is going and why it matters. (**Create clarity**)	4.65
2.	Values people by giving praise and recognition for achievement in ways that are meaningful to the recipients. (**Fully engage people**)	4.95
3.	Seeks input from district and store managers in critical areas of the business. (**Fully engage people**)	5.35
4.	Provides ongoing coaching and feedback for managers to grow. (**Serve others**)	6.10
5.	Works to keep everyone on the same page by sharing information and listening to feedback. (**Create clarity**)	6.25

Finally, we looked at the comments sections. The pattern that I saw was one of impatience—impatience in my conversations with people, always wanting to get on to the next thing. I guess that's pretty much true. I'm busy and don't have time to dawdle, but it seems as though

I am rushing through important conversations that I shouldn't be. At the conclusion of looking at the data, Coach Kay asked me for my analysis.

"I guess it's pretty clear that people respect and trust me for my passion, integrity, and courage. I feel good about that. The surprise to me is that I don't communicate as well as I thought I did. Apparently, I don't seek input or coach and develop people very well."

"Was that a blind spot for you, Denny?" Kay probed.

"It must be because I thought it was a strength. I suppose the good news is we uncovered it." I had to reflect on that one.

"What is your take on the feedback, Kay?" She had been through a lot of these, so I really was interested in her perspective.

"I concur with you, Denny. People really respect you for your work ethic, character, and courage. And, that's really good news. When leaders don't have those things, there's not much I can do to help." Coach Kay then asked me to draw a baseball diamond on a piece of paper. She provided me with another context for diamond leadership.

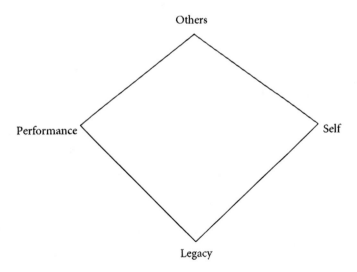

"Denny, in leadership, first base is about *self* leadership. It is about having integrity, courage, and passion for your work—like you do."

Kay continued the baseball lesson. "Second base is about *others*. Getting to second base is about serving and engaging others. The results are trust and commitment."

"Third base is about *performance*. When we put the right people in the right roles, coach for performance, and create clarity in our organizations, performance is the result."

"Getting to home plate is about creating a *legacy*. When we lead in such a way that achieves performance, and honors and develops people, we impact organizations and communities in a way that creates a legacy. That kind of leadership makes an impact. The rules of leadership are like the rules of baseball—you have to run the bases in order. If you haven't covered first base with self-leadership, you can't lead others effectively. If you don't engage others effectively at second base, you can't get to third base and achieve the levels of performance people are really capable of.

Baseball fan that I am, the metaphor made great sense to me.

"Based on the feedback from your 360 assessment, what base are you on Denny?"

Silence.

"First base," finally came out.

Chapter 6

Micro-Initiatives

An idea isn't worth that much. It's the execution of the idea that has value.

Joel Spolsky, CEO of Fog Creek Software

After taking a week to reflect on the feedback, the baseball metaphor that Kay used reminded me of the great St. Louis Cardinal, Albert Pujols, baseball's best hitter. Pujols goes into the clubhouse and watches videotapes after each of his at-bats. He uses that feedback to make adjustments in the next at-bat. His results speak for themselves. That reminder helped me get over being disappointed at the feedback and resolve to use it to my advantage.

"So, where do we go from here," I asked Coach Kay at the beginning of our next coaching session. I was eager to get on with taking action.

"Next, we identify two to three micro-initiatives. Micro-initiatives are targeted behaviors that, if performed consistently, will make the most difference in your development and overall performance."

"So," I responded, "our next job is to figure out which micro-initiatives are the right ones. It sounds like we have to do some strategic thinking."

"That's exactly right, Denny. The most important question for us to think through is this: what are the two to three behaviors that, if you did them consistently well, would most impact your performance as a regional manager and create balance?"

"Why just two to three," I wondered. "Based on my feedback, I'd say I need to do more."

"Great question, Denny. My experience is that busy people can't take on more than that. Trying to do more is to fall into the trap we are already in—doing too many things, none of them very well. I've found that people can make a big difference by taking on the right two to three and doing them consistently well." Kay's coaching made sense.

"Picking the right ones may be tough. Where do we start?"

"I recommend we just do some brainstorming, just start tossing ideas out and don't worry if they are the right ones; we can evaluate them later. Write them down on Post-It notes as they occur to you. I'll add some to the mix, if you don't mind."

It sounded as good as anything I would have come up with, so we brainstormed for about twenty minutes. I've done a lot of brainstorming before, and this was no different. We came up with some good ideas, some wacky ones, and some interesting ones. The cool thing to me was the next exercise—evaluating the ideas. Coach Kay had me draw a grid that had "impact" on one axis and "implementation" on another. It looked like this.

Implementation

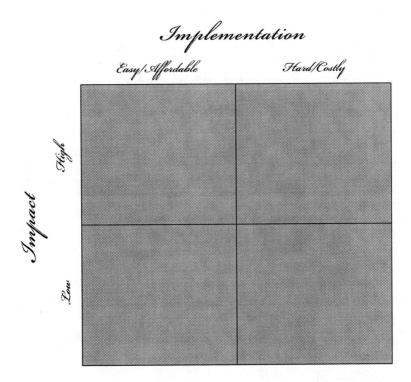

How Kay explained the process was to take each idea written on a Post-It note and evaluate it based on the two criteria. First, was the idea high or low impact, and second, was the idea easy or hard to implement. I made a mental note to use this process for other brainstorming exercises with my team.

There were three ideas that seemed to be high impact and do-able.

Create more clarity. Get everyone on the same page through better meetings and conference calls.

> *Engage my people more. Seek out their ideas on improving key aspects of the business. Be more approachable and patient and listen.*

> *Turn my weekly status meetings with my district managers into coaching sessions to further their development.*

"Those seem like great goals for your business objectives. I am wondering how they might help the balance issues." The coach posed an important question.

"I think saving time might be a by-product of some of these initiatives." Truthfully, I was blowing a little smoke. I was thinking more about the business objectives. But as I thought about it, there seemed to be some potential in what I was saying, so I continued. "If I can get the team on the same page with better meetings, it will save me time on the back end answering questions and redirecting people.

"Also, if I can turn my status meetings, time I am already spending with my district managers, into coaching sessions that develop them and reduce their reliance on me, which could definitely help. The third goal of engaging people more will take more time on the front end, but I think will improve the business and cause me to do less crisis management." As I was explaining it, it sounded pretty good.

"It sounds like you are getting clear about some issues that will help you become more effective. I'd like to work with you to make sure your goals are actionable."

"What do you mean?" I knew what actionable meant but wasn't sure where she was coming from.

"Let's take your third goal. Engage your people more and get their input. Generally, that's a great objective. We can make it actionable by doing two things—be specific about what input you are seeking and from whom, and then put it on your calendar."

"OK, I got it. So, a goal might be: get input from my district managers and key store managers on improving sales on the new product line."

"Right," Kay responded. "And, then make sure it gets on your calendar. Goals won't get executed until they get on your calendar."

"Makes sense. I think I am ready to go." I was ready to get off the phone and get back to work.

"If it's OK, I'd like to ask you about one more of your goals before we go." Kay was so good at asking permission to coach.

"Sure."

"Your goal of turning your status meetings into coaching sessions seems really smart to me. I'd like to hear more about how those will change."

"Well, right now, it's pretty much a review of the numbers—the performance metrics. We key in on the sub par numbers, and then I give them my best advice on what to do, based on my experience."

"How is that working?" Kay asked.

As I was explaining it to Kay, it occurred to me why that wasn't working. It's amazing how talking things through can help you discover solutions. "What is occurring to me as we're talking is that my telling them what to do isn't helping them grow or creating buy-in. People buy-in to their own solutions more than the solutions of others."

"That's an excellent observation, Denny. That's my experience too," Kay affirmed. "So, what will you do differently?"

"I'll do exactly what you are doing with me right now. I'll ask great questions to help them discover the solutions and offer my own advice when appropriate." The light bulbs were popping.

"Denny, I call that 'ask first, then tell' in my coaching model for exactly the reasons you stated."

"You have a coaching model? Would it be helpful to me?"

"I think so. I'll e-mail it to you when we're done with the call. We can talk about it when you are ready."

"Great." I was beginning to get excited.

"I think you've got a good sense of going forward. The last thing I'd like to leave you with is a tool called a weekly scorecard. I'll e-mail it to you. There are four sections to it. The idea here is to write at least one actionable item for each of your three goals in section one. In section two, write when you are going to perform each goal. Put them on your calendar. This will help you create new habits in the areas you've decided were important. In section three, jot down any resources or tools you may need for each task. For example, in your coaching goal, you could use the coaching model as a resource or tool to help you with that goal. Finally, at the end of the week, evaluate yourself on how you performed. Denny, I can't emphasize this enough. This is a big deal. It is the difference between good intentions and executing, and you know in business, execution is everything." Coach Kay made the last point with real emphasis.

She e-mailed me the form, and I created three actionable goals for the next week and e-mailed it back. I could see why the tool could appear deceiving in its simplicity but powerful if it helped create new habits.

Weekly Scorecard

Week of: March 18

Goal or Action	Times/Dates scheduled	Support/Tools	Self-rating (1-10)
Hold a conference call with my district managers and get input on improving the quality of the calls so they are shorter and everyone gets the clarity they need and a chance to be heard.	Mar 25	Have my assistant set up the call. Communicate ahead of time so district managers come prepared to give input.	
Coach Bill Evans (DM) on improving the effectiveness of his store visits. His approach is too much like the "Soup Nazi."	Mar 22	Use Coach Kay's coaching model. Review it with her before I coach Bill.	
Have an evening "town hall" session with all store managers during my visit to the Kansas City market. Get their input on improving sales of the new product lines.	Mar 20	Ask for a volunteer to take notes in the meeting for follow-up purposes. I hate doing that!	

Amazing! After going through this simple exercise, I felt like I had a pretty good game plan for going forward that seemed really do-able.

I knew staying consistent would be really important.

Chapter 7

Trouble at Home

If Mama ain't happy, ain't nobody happy.

Lindsey O'Connor

I was feeling pretty good about things since Kay helped me identify some specific initiatives to work on. They seemed like high-leverage items that could make a big impact.

A week later, I was having one of those days where I was running late for everything. I had some specific objectives to accomplish for the day, and other things just came up. They always do. I had several things to do before my Kansas City trip and was really hustling to get them all done. At four o'clock, an impromptu meeting was called by Brad Blessman, the chief operating officer and Number Two person in the company. As an organization, we were running over our budget in payrolls costs, one of the largest budget items for any retailer. He was in a foul mood and wanted to crack the whip and get the numbers back in line. He wasn't really interested in any explanations.

As the meeting was wearing on, I became aware that it was past five o'clock, and I had made a commitment to meet Susan at Ronnie's basketball game. I didn't have a very good track record lately at making it to the kids' events and was feeling pretty lousy about it. Susan hadn't said much, but I knew she was becoming unhappy about it. She knew how busy I was at work and had been understanding about our lack of time together, but when it came to the kids, she was less understanding. I was not living up to her expectations—or my own for that matter.

When the meeting finally ended, I shot out of there like a mean-spirited put-down out of Ann Coulter's mouth—with force and purpose.

Murphy's Law was at work. Rush hour traffic was worse than usual. When I finally got to the game—late in the second half—Susan all but ignored me. She was clearly unhappy with me. The rest of the week didn't get any better. My body and spirit felt tired.

That weekend, I decided to practice the Diamond Leadership Model at home and "Act with Courage" by having a conversation with Susan. I didn't really know what to say, but instinctively I knew I needed to shoot straight with her about how I was feeling about life, work, and marriage, and give her the opportunity to do the same. Frankly, I was dreading it, but knew I needed to do it—and soon.

So, we talked. My hope of having a great conversation evaporated quickly. I didn't handle it well. I started off talking about my feelings, finally let her have her say, and when her feelings about my priorities became hard to hear, I got defensive. And, it went downhill from there. Somewhere in the conversation, I shared with her that I had a coach that was trying to help me with my job so that I could create more balance and be available for my family. She uncharacteristically took a shot at me about not needing a coach for work, but needing a coach for home. That kind of aggressiveness was totally unlike her and was a clear indication that things were worse than I thought. I felt like some boneheaded Dr. Phil guest and even more deflated.

The next coaching conversation with Kay was an SOS—a call of distress. I was still really upset about my conversation with Susan.

"Tell me about the conversation."

"I don't know, Kay. I went into it with the best of intentions, but it went downhill fast."

Kay listened. "Tell me more about it."

I explained how I decided to go for it—to have the conversation I had been avoiding, but that I probably talked too much, listened too little, and got defensive when Susan expressed her feelings.

"Denny, I can sense your discouragement. But I want you to know that I admire the fact that you had the courage to have the difficult conversation. Challenging conversations like this require courage and some pretty advanced skills to navigate them. I can help you with the skills."

"That's great, Kay," I responded, "because leaving it like it is now is not acceptable."

"I'll e-mail you a model I use for having difficult conversations, where the objectives are to solve the problem and maintain and even enhance the relationship. It works both in our business and personal lives. Then, we can go through the model and even practice the conversation. How does that sound?" the coach inquired.

"That sounds great, Kay, but the more pressing need for me is to solve the problem that has led to where we are."

"Tell me more about that," Kay responded.

"I botched the conversation with Susan, but the real problem is why we even had to have the conversation. It's the ongoing problem of working too many hours and not spending enough time with her and the kids." It didn't take a PhD in root cause analysis to understand that the state of my marriage was a symptom of my not being there enough.

"To what degree are the micro-initiatives you've been working on making a difference in your work-life balance?" Kay inquired.

"They are all on the right track. But having better meetings, coaching and delegating more, and getting input and engaging people more are all long-term propositions with more long-term payback."

"I hear you, but I might challenge you on one of those items. Doing more delegating with the right people can have a more immediate impact on freeing up some time, Denny. What do you think?"

"I guess that is one thing that could have a quicker pay-off. In fact, my boss' feedback was that I do too much myself." The feedback from Steve in our first meeting just came back to me. "Let me give some thought to what I can get off my plate and discuss them in our next call. I have to tell you, though; I feel a real sense of urgency about this."

After more discussion about my sense of urgency to get my work-life balance under control, Kay suggested a "feed-forward session." Except for the fact that I had no idea what that meant, it sounded really great to me.

Chapter 8

Feed-Forward

Life can only be understood backwards; but it must be lived forwards.

Soren Kierkegaard

"Feed-forward is where we seek input and ideas from people you respect about solving a problem or how to handle a big challenge. Where feedback is valuable in looking at your current habits and practices, feed-forward takes out the judgment aspect and starts with a clean slate." Often, Kay's explanation of things seemed so common-sense and left me wondering why I hadn't thought of it myself. This was one of those occasions.

Coach Kay's explanation of how to do a feed-forward session was just as straightforward. The process was for me to invite several people to a meeting and ask for their ideas on the challenge I was experiencing. The criteria for selecting these people were that I trusted them with sharing the details of my challenge, believed them capable of confidentiality, and respected their insights and level of excellence regarding the work-life challenge. Furthermore, they were willing and available. The coach indicated that it was critical that I let people know exactly what the challenge was and what input I was looking for from them, and give them advance notice to get their thoughts together. She also recommended that she facilitate the session so I could focus on listening and recording the ideas that appealed to me.

On the day of the feed-forward session, I was surprised that I was nervous. The session was a conference call with four people, plus Kay and me. None of them were current colleagues. I wasn't comfortable sharing this information with people I worked with. Kay suggested that in this kind of session, the caliber of the people was what mattered, more than who they worked for. The four were Bruce Pella, Ginny Berkman, Bob Emerson, and Harry Rose.

I kicked the session off by thanking the people there for their time, their willingness to share their ideas, and their confidentiality. I realized that my nervousness was because I was exposing my weaknesses and my personal life. I then introduced Coach Kay, who explained how the session would go. Simply put, each person, one by one, would get the opportunity to share their ideas with me, ask questions, and explore options. Each person would get about fifteen minutes. My job was to listen, answer questions, ask clarifying questions, and be open-minded.

Kay asked me to e-mail everyone a week ahead of time a paragraph about my challenge, specifically what input I was looking for and what things I have tried to solve the problem.

Following is what I e-mailed to the group.

> **My Challenge:**
> I am working too many hours, and it is adversely impacting my marriage and family life. I don't know how to work fewer hours and accomplish what I need to in order to be successful and grow in my job as regional manager. My career objective is to get to the next level in my organization and have a family life. It's not working.
>
> **The Input I am looking for:**
> Your best practices for balancing being an effective leader and having a quality family life. I am not looking for time management theory but what works for you. Thanks for your help!!
>
> **What I have tried:**
> What I have tried is working more hours. It hasn't improved my region's performance; but it has been successful in compromising my family life. I am open to ideas!

Bruce Pella went first. Bruce was an executive and a friend who used to work for The Cooking Store and left to start his own business. "First, Denny, I want to thank you for inviting me to this session. I consider it a privilege to be asked to support a colleague I value as much as you. And, hey, I hope to learn something myself."

Bruce was always such a gentleman. "The thing that works best for me to achieve effectiveness and balance is to keep the main thing the main thing. That may seem like a blinding flash of the obvious, but the key is in the execution. Here's what I have done. It's kind of a three-step process. First, I gave a lot of thought about what my main things were—my priorities. As it relates to my job, I thought about what truly drives my business and gets results, and then I identified the activities that were critical to achieving those results. I had to push hard to identify what they really were. When I took a hard look at it, I found it to be a shorter list than I thought it would be. Not everything we do drives performance, and if an activity was not a performance-driver, I knocked it off the list. What remained is what I believe Dr. Covey calls "High Leverage Activities."

Bruce paused and then continued, "The second step is weekly planning. On Sunday night, about nine o'clock, I spend about twenty to thirty minutes planning my week. Sunday night works for me because, mentally, the weekend is over, and my mind starts gravitating to work anyway. So, I just go with it. What I do during that time is identify my high-leverage activities and schedule them. Most of them are communication sessions, planning, coaching and developing people, and building relationships with customers and vendors. Putting them on the calendar is the key. When it's on the calendar, it becomes a commitment, and I am fanatical about keeping my commitments. If I have a one-on-one session with one of my people, I refuse to break it unless it is a true emergency. The key I've found is discipline and consistency. Since I started doing this faithfully, I spend much more time doing what matters and much less time doing what doesn't.

"The third step is to evaluate myself at the end of the week on the execution of those HLAs. I give my self a score of 1–10 at the end of the week and make course corrections when I see slippage in execution. For me, Denny, it's about focus and discipline. It has made a big difference in both performance and optimizing my time."

Kay asked me what my key take-away was. "It sounds like Bruce uses something like the weekly scorecard you've suggested. I should give it a try."

Bruce's Yoda-like response was, "There is no try—there is only do."

Ginny was next. Ginny is a marketing executive with another company and a friend from church. "Denny, I also want to thank you for inviting me, and I really appreciated Bruce's thoughts. My thoughts are going to be similar to his but different."

"Similar but different sounds very Yogi Berra-ish," I couldn't help but responding.

"It probably is," Ginny laughed. "What works for me is to do what Bruce talked about in scheduling time and guarding it jealously. Where my feedback is different from Bruce's is in its application. My recommendation is to do the same thing with your family. In fact, I highly recommend that busy married people date their spouse."

"Date their spouse," I repeated somewhat dumbly.

"Yes. My husband and I have two dates per month. Once it's on the calendar, only an emergency moves it. It is an ironclad commitment. And—this may sound like a little thing, but I believe it is a big thing—7:00 is 7:00, and 8:00 is 8:00. It is a respect thing."

"That sounds good, but sometimes I end up in late meetings about important business."

"More important than your marriage?"

"That's not fair. I hear that enough from Susan."

"You asked for my honest feedback. I'm giving it to you."

"OK. Thanks. But really, how do you leave a meeting without being rude or teeing off your boss?" I really wanted to know that one.

"What works for me is to tell people, 'Excuse me, I'm leaving. I have a date with my husband.' I've found that people respect that. If you work in a culture that doesn't respect family time, leave. It's not worth it." That was blunt and made me glad that I invited people from outside the company who could say that.

"Thank you, Ginny. I am not sure the culture is the problem. I have to own this one." I remembered what Coach Kay had said earlier about how our behavior is what demonstrates our values and priorities, not our words.

Next up was Bob. Bob was an executive with a manufacturing company and a friend. We've had coffee many times and talked business and family stuff. Bob is a fun and bright guy. "Denny, I think I have a pretty good handle on your leadership style—a bit of a control freak—so, I have one word for you: let go."

"'Let go' is two words," I shot back.

"See, I told you, you're controlling my spiel," Bob laughed. "Seriously, Denny, what I want to share is *letting go*. It's a lesson I've had to learn. I once received feedback that I was giving too much direction. I would give assignments, and then follow people around and tell them how to do them, and then take over when it wasn't being done like I wanted. I was not only spending too much time doing other people's work, I wasn't letting them try on their own, fail occasionally, and grow. It was lose-lose. Give people the outcomes you are looking for and let them do their jobs. Coach them appropriately, and let them grow."

Coach Kay affirmed what Bob said and reminded that we would be reviewing a coaching model she'd given me.

Harry was next. Harry is a lifelong friend. We went to school together, and he is a teacher and a coach. He also does a lot of work with youth in his church. He has a lot of responsibility and is incredibly busy.

"Denny, I want to echo every one else's sentiments about being asked to help. My thoughts are going to be about the value of time. So, my question to you is what value do you put on your time?"

"I don't know. Since I'm not on the clock, I don't look at it that way. I guess I could break my salary down to an hourly rate."

"That's one way to look at it," Harry said. "Let me ask you this—what are you being held accountable for?"

"A lot of things. People. Costs. Customer service. Sales."

"Bottom-line it for me," Harry pushed. What are you most being held accountable for that is most quantifiable?"

"Sales. Specifically, my goal is a two-million-dollar sales increase for my region this year."

"Good. Break it down for me. If you work roughly fifty hours per week towards a two-million-dollar objective, what is your hourly goal?"

Fortunately, I had a calculator on my desk. "OK, if I work about twenty-five hundred hours a year," I said, calculating out loud, "and divide that into two million dollars, then my hourly goal would be eight hundred dollars in increased sales."

"Every hour of the working year," Harry added. "It's just one way of looking at it, but the point is to understand that every one of those twenty-five hundred hours that is spent not working toward that end, you are falling behind. Because there are administrative things that go with the job that take you away from driving sales, figure you have two thousand hours per year to drive sales. If my math is correct, that is about thousand dollars per hour as a goal."

The value of my time was starting to sink in.

"One way to look at it," Harry continued, "is every hour of your working time has a one thousand dollar objective. So, spend every hour as if you were spending a thousand dollars of your own money. Think cash. It will cause you to spend your time differently."

"That's a great insight Harry. I never really thought about the value of time that way."

For the first time in awhile, Kay chimed in. "Harry, what is a skill or discipline you would recommend to Denny to turn that concept into action?" It was vintage Kay. "Turning knowing into doing is the key to growth," I have heard her say to me many times.

Harry responded quickly. "It boils down to two disciplines. The first is being intentional about your time. Bruce and Ginny have given great advice in that area. The second discipline is that discipline of saying no to requests for your time that do not drive your business or serve your accountabilities."

"Easier said than done" I said a little cynically.

"Absolutely true," Harry responded. "Let me explain what works for me. There are two ways to say no. First, is the direct approach. 'No' or 'No, thank you.' For example, someone asks you to come to a meeting or participate in a committee. The direct way is to simply say, 'No, thank you.' You can state your reason for saying no or not. It's up to you."

"And, the indirect way?" I asked.

"I realize it's not always easy or appropriate using the direct no, like with your boss. The keys to the indirect no are to ask questions and explore alternatives."

"Give me an example," I said.

"Sure. Your boss says, 'Denny, I want you to come to a meeting this afternoon about customer service. I really want you to be there.' And, you have a one-on-one session scheduled with one of your direct reports. What do you do?"

"I usually change my schedule. It happens all the time."

"What is the impact?" Harry asked.

"My direct report feels devalued, and I end up in a meeting and unhappy about it."

"How could you have said no to that meeting?" Harry pressed.

"I guess I could have told the boss that I have an important meeting scheduled with a direct report and rescheduling will give the wrong message. I could have asked him some questions about the purpose of the meeting and what contribution he needed from me. Someone else may have been able to go in my place." I was seeing how it was possible to say no the indirect way.

"Great. You're on the right track, Denny. You won't win them all, but push back when you need to."

Harry, like the others, gave me invaluable advice. I felt humbled to be the recipient of their time and experience. I made a note to remember to use feed-forward sessions with my own team to help managers solve problems and simply share best practices.

Chapter 9

Serving Through Coaching

List the qualities of a great leader and then of a great coach and you'll end up with the same list.

Sandy Hinderliter

I was looking forward to my trip to Kansas City, partly because it was still pretty tense at home and partly because I was going try out some new coaching skills. My typical visit to a market would be to spend two to three days visiting stores with the district manager of that market and then conducting a half-day, or occasionally a full-day, meeting with all the managers from that market.

The store visits usually consisted of me going through the store operations with the manager and district manager and then giving them feedback and telling them what needed to be done to fix any issues they were having. Word had gotten back to me that I was considered a practitioner of "seagull management": fly in, crap on people, and fly back out. That seemed a little blown out of proportion, but based on my 360 feedback, maybe I wasn't developing my district managers or store managers by being the one to point out problems and offer the solutions. I was doing too much "telling."

The meetings with the managers probably weren't much different. I did too much reporting of the numbers and too much lecturing on what needed to be done. The entire burden was on me to conduct the meeting, identify what the problems were, and tell them what the solutions were. What I probably was doing well was the recognition piece. I made it a point to celebrate achievements in the districts. Unwittingly, in the meetings, I made the district manager too much of a bystander while I took over. It was the same as the store visits. With some coaching from Coach Kay, my plan was to let the district manager take the lead in the store visits and coach them on developing the store managers, and in the district meetings, again let the district manager take the lead and work with them to engage the managers in identifying challenges and solutions.

Before the first store visit, I spent some time on the phone with the district manager, Maria Martinez. I was upfront with her about how I thought my visits were not as effective as they could be and described how I would like to let her take the lead in the store visits and in the meeting. I shared with her my ideas and asked for her feedback. I could sense her excitement about taking ownership. It made me wonder why I hadn't thought of it before. We were scheduled to do four half-day store visits in the first two days and then have a one-day meeting on day three to create some different dynamics than we've had before.

Before the first store visit, I e-mailed Maria a coaching model that Kay had shared with me. I thought we would use it to turn the store visits into coaching sessions rather than the "seagull" sessions they were perceived to be. She laughed at the seagull reference. Apparently, she'd heard it before.

What I thought we might do is spend a couple of hours observing and then sit down with the managers and review the Big Three (as we called them): Performance (metrics), People, and Operations. The difference is how we go through the Big Three. Instead of how we see them and telling the manager what to do about them, we get their perspective on each of the three and their ideas on what actions to take. We would use the coaching tool Kay sent me.

Performance Coaching Planning Tool

1. **Set the tone**
   - Check-in at a personal level.
   - Begin with merits.
   - Praise, then pause.

   Notes:

2. **Transition to concerns**
   - No buts or howevers!
   - State clearly the performance issue or gap.
   - Deal with behaviors and facts, never the person.

   Notes:

3. **Discuss and determine causes**
   - Ask open ended questions.
   - Listen—genuine listening.
   - Cut through any smokescreens. Keep dialoguing.

   Notes:

4. **Seek a solution**
   - Ask for a solution. People are committed to their own solutions!!
   - Advise if necessary.
   - Offer any needed support.
   - Confirm understanding and agreement. Play back!

   Notes:

5. **Establish a follow-up**
   - Set a time and date.
   - Step out and let them do their job.
   - Step back in and praise or coach as necessary.

   Notes:

Maria expressed her enthusiasm for the process. She indicated that the visits would be more constructive, the managers would take more ownership of solutions, and the development of the managers would be accelerated. Maria suggested that I do the coaching for the first two store visits, so she could learn from observing, and then she take the lead in the second two visits. I started to push back, thinking it would be to her benefit if she did all the coaching; but, I chose to accept her idea so that she felt listened to and that her input mattered. Ordinarily, I would have pushed for my idea and won the debate—and lost her sense of ownership. It felt like a step forward.

Before we went to the first store, it was bothering me a little that Maria's role might be too passive in the first visits. While I was OK with her listening and observing, I thought she should be more engaged, so I created a simple Word document she could use to give me feedback on my coaching. She would learn from being asked to observe the coaching process and then give me feedback. In that this was new to me, I would benefit too. I would just have to put my ego aside. Then I could use the same feedback instrument when I observed Maria and the other DMs and gave them feedback.

I created a document, sent it to Kay for her feedback, and got a couple of recommendations for refinement, along with a big "Attaboy."

The observer used the following instrument by checking yes or no on the specific coaching behaviors. They then should give at least two specifics on what the coach did well and a couple of things to fine-tune. My thought was that two people were getting the chance to coach—the coach and the observer. The observer would give feedback privately after the coaching session.

Performance Coaching Feedback Tool

Skills Performed	Y *or* N
1. Set the tone - Check-in at a personal level. - Begin with merits. - Praise, then pause. **2. Transition to concerns** - No buts or howevers! - State clearly the performance issue or gap. - Deal with behaviors and facts, never the person. **3. Discuss and determine causes** - Ask open ended questions. - Listen—genuine listening. - Cut through any smokescreens. Keep dialoguing. **4. Seek a solution** - Ask for a solution. People are committed to their own solutions!! - Advise if necessary. - Offer any needed support. - Confirm understanding and agreement. Play back! **5. Establish a follow-up** - Set a time and date. - Step out and let them do their job. - Step back in and praise or coach as necessary.	

Did Well	Fine Tune
1.	1.
2.	2.

The first two coaching visits and coaching sessions went well. The first one I did was good, the second was better. I could sense that there was real dialogue taking place with the manager, and in both cases, they came up with some solutions to the performance challenges. I added my own ideas, but not until they offered theirs. At the end, we agreed on some specific action items for the manager to take. After the sessions, Maria gave me some very specific feedback on my coaching. The cool thing was it helped me, and she learned from the process of observing and giving feedback. The simple tool I created was tremendously valuable. I was feeling pretty full of myself.

As well as the first two visits and coaching sessions went, I was more excited about what happened in the next two. Maria took the lead working with the store managers, and I was the observer.

The third visit went really well. Maria was a good student. The last one was nothing short of extraordinary. The store manager for that visit, Shawn Hanaday, is really bright and creative. He can also be defensive and stubborn. He loves his own ideas and resists other people's ideas, including ours. I was so proud of how Maria led the conversation. We met at the end of the day, after spending the afternoon there.

"Shawn thanks for letting Denny and me spend this time with you and your staff."

"Sure," Shawn responded a little tentatively.

"One of the things I love about coming to this store is the passion you have for the business. It shows with your team. I know your customers feel really valued. I saw it in their interactions with you and the team. The other thing I am impressed with is how clean and organized your store is. In fact, I overheard one of your customers making that comment to the lady she was with. It sounded like they really appreciated it, and so do I." Maria paused.

Shawn looked at her for a couple of seconds. She waited.

"Well, uh, thank you, Maria, I really appreciate that. We work hard here and love what we do." Shawn's demeanor seemed to soften a little.

"It shows, Shawn," Maria responded.

She paused again. I could see that she was taking a few seconds and letting Shawn bask in the compliments. No buts or howevers!

"Shawn, we talked about the first of the Big Three this morning before we got started, the performance metrics. What I thought we might talk about now is people. Tell me how your staff is doing."

"I have a great staff. They are passionate about the business, just like I am." Shawn was clearly proud of his team.

"That's what I see, too, Shawn. What I am wondering is how can they become even better?" Maria was gently pushing.

Shawn was silent. Maria waited.

"I don't know, Maria. We're all really good at customer service." Shawn was resisting her invitation.

"I agree. Your store is one of the best in the district at customer service. How about sales?" Again, it was an invitation for Shawn to identify the opportunity.

"Yeah, I suppose we could get better at sales. Our average sale per customer could be better. The numbers we reviewed this morning put us in the middle of the district." He was coming around.

"How do you feel about that?"

"I'd like to be better. You know me—I want to do a great job."

"That's one of the things I really appreciate about you, Shawn." Maria kept affirming. "So, how would you assess the sales skills of your team?" She was inviting more self-assessment.

"Well, we're probably a little weak on consultative selling. We have a lot of product knowledge and could do more recommending to the customer." Shawn was coming around more.

"I agree with that observation. During my time here this morning, I observed several missed opportunities to make product recommendations. How can we improve those skills?" She was now shifting to solutions, knowing that he would be more bought into his solutions. It was a beautiful thing to see. Maria guided Shawn through identifying a problem and coming up with his own solutions. His key recommendation was to do some sales training with the team and some role-playing.

Maria added her own recommendation that they have an observer give feedback for each of the practice sessions.

The outcome was that Shawn walked away with a plan that was his—he owned it, and Maria supported it. The feedback session I had with Maria afterward was that she did an amazing job setting the tone for the conversation and guiding Shawn to identify the problem and the solutions. The fine-tuning suggestion I offered was to observe the training. It occurred to me that based on Shawn's own sales skills, she shouldn't assume that his training would be effective. Because it was an investment of additional payroll dollars, she should be there to observe and coach as necessary.

Maria and I were both pretty fired up at how well the session went with Shawn. I was even more jazzed about making the store visits like she just conducted the norm and not the exception to the rule. If we could accomplish that, we could really start to develop people and create more of a sense of ownership in the region. I was pumped!

As Coach Kay said, one of the best ways to serve people is to teach and coach. The individual, the customer, and the organization all win.

Chapter 10

Engaging the Team

Without involvement, there is no commitment. Mark it down, asterisk it, circle it, underline it. No involvement, no commitment.

Stephen R. Covey

The next day, Maria and I would convene a meeting with all managers in her district. We created the agenda together and agreed she would conduct part of it, and I would conduct part. That was a departure from the past—my agenda, my meeting. The part I did want to do was to engage the managers in some brainstorming about how to increase sales of the new product line of upscale cookware. I was excited about using the brainstorming techniques that I learned from Kay.

Maria did a nice job of running the morning session. Her primary objectives were to explain in some detail new marketing and operational initiatives. In fact, she probably did a better job than I would have. She patiently fielded questions and concerns that people always have with new programs. Again, it made me realize that I had a talented leader in Maria, with a lot of potential that I hadn't been developing. Her growth was important to the growth of the district and, from a selfish perspective, would help me to spend less time handling problems in the district and more time with my family. I was beginning to see a flicker of light at the end of the tunnel.

In the afternoon, I started off the brainstorming session by identifying the challenge—to maximize sales of the new upscale cookware product line. I explained to the store managers that they were in the best position to come up with some strategies to ramp up our sales because they know their teams and their customers. That may have been the first time they'd heard that from me. Usually, it was my program and plan I was pumping up.

Next, I gave on a flipchart the ground rules for brainstorming I learned from a mentor at my previous company and from Coach Kay.

- Clearly define the problem or objective—and the business impact.
- Go for a quantity of ideas.
- Set a time limit.
- Don't judge ideas (at first).
- Write down everything (using Post-It notes).
- Say your idea out loud and put it on the board.
- Build on each others' ideas.
- Evaluate ideas at the end.

Often, I've seen brainstorming done with someone acting as a scribe. The problem I've seen with that is that the scribe can edit what people say, may have a hard time keeping up, and takes themselves out of the brainstorming. Using Post-It notes lets everyone write their own ideas, and the Post-Its are mobile. That is valuable when we evaluate ideas.

I split the ten people into two groups of five. I challenged them with coming up with sixty ideas in forty minutes. Pushing brainstorming groups with an extreme number of ideas makes them get past the obvious solutions. They groaned.

"Come on, you can do it. You people are smart and creative," I encouraged.

They began. Maria and I were observers. Our job was to make sure they followed the ground rules, and to help them if they got stuck. Both of us had to step in with our group and remind them of the ground rule "no judging ideas" in the brainstorming phase. Otherwise, it was a fun process to observe. People were really engaged in putting ideas forward. Often, one idea was the spark for another. I overheard "naked cooking demonstrations" come out of Maria's group and then uproarious laughter. Interestingly, the group that laughed the most and seemed to be having the most fun produced the most ideas.

At the end of the brainstorming session, I asked the groups to do one more thing before we moved into the evaluation session. It was to see if any ideas combined to create a more powerful idea. My explanation was, "Think about chocolate and peanut butter." What happened when those two things were combined? "Reese's Peanut Butter Cup" was the answer. A whole new product came from the simple combination of two current products. Ideas are the same way.

At the end of that session, we moved into the evaluation phase. I asked the groups to place each Post-It note on the flipchart pages I prepared, where the evaluation model was drawn. I explained the process of evaluating them based on the impact of the idea and the ease or difficulty of implementation, which could include cost factors.

Again, it was fun to observe the dialogue that went into the evaluation process. People were engaged—and that engagement stands a much better chance of turning into ownership than my plan would have. What a difference from the other meetings I'd been conducting.

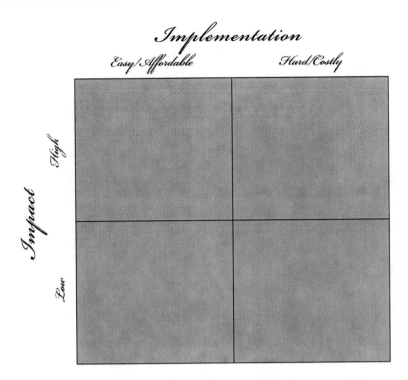

In the end, there were several ideas that fell into the "easy to implement" and "high impact" quadrant. The biggest thing was that they were their ideas. Maria took on the assignment of working with the managers to prioritize and execute the ideas. As Kay says with turning learning into doing, "It's all about execution." One of the ideas was to have a fun sales contest and invite me to the winning store to cook a gourmet dinner for the entire team. The word was out that I am a gourmet cook. I think it's because I am the one that tells everyone. I couldn't help but chuckle. Shooting my mouth off came back to me again. Remembering "serve others" from the Diamond Leadership Model, I enthusiastically agreed.

Chapter 11

Everything Is a Priority

If everything is a priority, nothing is a priority.

David Allen

We were starting to make real progress in my region. My coaching skills were improving, and so were the skills of my district managers. I was engaging them more, tapping into their ideas and talents, and they were doing the same with their store managers. I was beginning to see the metrics improve a little in my region, and we seemed to be moving the needle on some important intangibles like morale, trust, and teamwork also. I realized that it was just a beginning, but it seemed that we were starting to shift from managing people to leading people. My sense is that it is the difference between controlling and empowering people.

Each quarter, I meet for two days with my six district managers. The meetings are for evaluating our business, planning, discussing challenges, sharing best practices, and recognition of achievement. As we were wrapping up the first day of our meeting at the end of the first quarter, I said as a closing comment, "We have some great momentum going, let's stay focused!" I am a big believer in focus, and it was intended to be a rallying cry like, "Let's win one for the Gipper!" or "Remember the Titans!" Something inspiring. I walked out of there thinking I had the team fired up and the next day would be even better.

We were going to get together for dinner later on that evening at the hotel we were staying at. As I headed down in the elevator for dinner, Mel Nielson, one of the district managers, got on the elevator from the floor he was on. I said something like, "Great ending to the first day wasn't it?" Mel looked at the floor and didn't say anything. That was unlike Mel because he usually says what's on his mind. He is honest to a fault, and I like that about him.

Finally, he looked at me and said, "Not really."

"What are you talking about?" I was stunned.

Our elevator arrived at the first floor where the restaurant was, and we walked off. "It was a good meeting, Denny," Mel said. "And, we all feel great about the good things going on. We do have some momentum going. We're excited about it. It was your last comment about staying focused that didn't sit well."

I started to get defensive but remembered the great implied question an old mentor taught me. He said when you need to listen for understanding, start with "tell me more about that." So, I did, and Mel told me more. The message was that it's hard to focus when everything is a priority. Mel indicated that those of us at corporate were the problem, me included. The message was clear: too many priorities, too many initiatives, too many numbers to track, too much information coming from the corporate office. It was hard for district and store managers to know what really was important.

I thanked Mel for shooting straight with me and reflected on it that evening. As I thought about it, my third micro-initiative created after reviewing my 360 feedback assessment was gaining more clarity. I had work to do.

The next day at the meeting, I told the group about the conversation with Mel and thanked him publicly for speaking up on behalf of the team. I gave the others the opportunity to weigh in. The message remained the same. I decided the best way to get at this problem was to work backwards by starting with what they needed to know to do their jobs with a high level of excellence. So, I asked them to go through an exercise with me. What I wanted to accomplish was to ask them, on behalf of their store managers specifically, what is it they need to be clear about so they could focus on the things that had the most impact on their business. The question I wrote on the flipchart was:

"What are the top five things store managers need to be clear about?"

They listed about twelve items, and then I asked them to prioritize. This was the final list.

- What is the big picture and the company's direction?"
- What are the real priorities?
- What are the most important metrics?
- How are we doing?
- What is changing and why?

I thanked the district managers for their input and told them I would give some thought on how to help create more focus from my end. On my trip back home, three things occurred to me.

First, I needed some clarity on what the real priorities were. The district managers had a point. If everything is a priority, then nothing is. That seemed to be an organizational issue. My job as the leader of my region was to first seek clarity for myself. The second thing was the metrics question. I understood where they were coming from. We try to focus on too many measures. Not all metrics are true indicators of success. That was one I needed to discuss with my boss and his boss. Third, I realized that every communication was an opportunity to create clarity—in meetings, conference calls, one-on-one sessions with district managers, store visits, and written communications.

At the next leadership meeting with senior management and my peers, I shared the feedback from the session with my district managers. The other regional managers agreed that their store managers felt like we had them constantly drinking from a fire hose. The dialogue was productive and it took several meetings, but the outcome was a good one. We made some decisions about what the real priorities were, at least for now, and whittled down the list of metrics we would hold them accountable for to the ones that really mattered.

It was a lesson to me that when people of courage speak up, as Mel Nielson did, and when leadership listens, the team or organization wins.

With Coach Kay's assistance, I put together a weekly communication template that I use as part of my newly adopted Sunday-night weekly planning.

Weekly Communication Plan

Communication	Key Message	Audience Targeted	Date Planned	Channel (in person, one-on-one, team meeting, e-mail, written letter, etc.)
What are the goals' priorities?				
What are the key metrics? What have we achieved?				
How are we doing? Who should I be giving feedback to?				
What is changing and why?				
What is the big picture? Where are we going?				

Over time, this tool helped me get better and more consistent at delivering the right messages to the right people, using the right channel. I knew that clarity was important for people to be able to focus on the right things and be able to make decisions on a day-to-day basis that were appropriate for the business. I realized in my business, the real test of clarity is not how clear it is at the top of the mountain, but at the bottom, where front-line people meet the customer.

Chapter 12

Beating Dead Horses

"Death by Meeting"

A book by Patrick Lencioni. The title says it all.

As a regional manager, I enjoy being out in the field more than I enjoy being in the corporate office. In the field, people are more fun and authentic. That's where business is really conducted. In the corporate office, there seems to be more personal agendas, and the place those agendas show up the most is in meetings.

One Monday morning, I found myself in one of those meetings. It was our weekly leadership meeting, and I was sitting there wondering if I would rather be here in this meeting or getting a prostate examination at home plate of Busch Stadium with forty thousand spectators. Tough call; I could go either way on it.

This meeting, like so many others, was painful. Here we are talking about the same stuff, every week, not really making any decisions or coming up with actionable items. We are masters of beating dead horses. The whinnying stopped a long time ago. Yet, here we are, debating the same stuff.

If it weren't so painful, it would be comical to sit back and just watch. It's like the movie *Groundhog Day* with Bill Murray. It's the same day, over and over.

Brad Blessman, the COO, is leading the meeting. Brad has great business instincts, but he also has the gift of consistently turning two-hour meetings into three-hour meetings. That's where we were going with this one. We invariably get buried in the minutiae, or the "peach fuzz," as one of my colleagues is fond of saying. Brad has a stack of reports he brings to the meeting that is as tall as Austin Powers' Mini-Me. He also likes to debate issues ad nauseum and is slow to decide anything.

Ben Simmons, director of IT, and Art Jackson, one of the regional managers, are arguing about the performance of the computer systems in the stores. They are important because they serve as the cash register and the system that tracks inventory, payroll, and a host of other administrative and reporting functions. Neither one is listening to the other's perspective. They are talking *at* each other. This is one of the dead horses we keep beating. The system is outdated and needs fixing, not continuous debate. It's a matter of making an investment decision about an important business tool for the store managers. It's one of those things that drive me crazy, when corporate people think the field operations, where the customers are, are there to serve them, rather than the other way around.

My boss, Steve Gillman, is engaged in a sidebar conversation with Sue Pearl, director of marketing. Tom Wolfe, another regional manager, is fidgeting. I can predict with complete certainty that he will head out to the men's room in the next three minutes. Karen Downing, the CFO, is sitting next to me. She's six months pregnant and looking miserable. She leans over to me and whispers, "I think I'm having contractions. I should go call my doctor."

"Funny thing," I whispered back, "You've been having contractions in these meetings for about three months." We both chuckled.

Bill Newbold, the HR director, has his Blackberry down on his lap, checking e-mail. Apparently, he is under the delusion that he is being coy and everyone can't see what he is doing. It annoys Steve Gillman to death, so every once in a while he'll ask Bill a question when he knows he's doing the e-mail thing. It's all so predictable.

I was looking around the room trying to calculate the cost of this waste of time. The ten people in the meeting were executives or senior managers, and if you broke their salaries down to an hourly rate, we probably averaged about $75 per hour in the room. We were pushing three hours in the meeting. The whole meeting wasn't a waste, but probably two hours were. So, my quick calculation was $75 x ten people x two wasted hours = $1500.00. That's the direct cost of being there, and it doesn't factor in what important work isn't being done because of the meeting. The thing is, we do it every week.

The meeting was supposed to end at 4:30, and now it was pushing 5:30. Susan and I had instituted date night every two weeks as a result of the feed-forward session. It was actually helping restore our wounded relationship. Tonight was date night, and I promised to be home by 6:00. This was a moment of truth. It was time to step up and make the right choice.

I didn't hesitate. I grabbed my files and stood up. The conversation stopped and all eyes moved to me.

"Please excuse me, but I have to go. This meeting is running an hour over the scheduled time, and I have a family commitment that I need to keep." I walked out. I can't remember anyone doing that before. My hands were sweating, and my heart was pounding. I looked straight ahead as I walked out, to avoid the stare, or glare, from Brad.

I got in the car, called Susan to tell her I was on my way, and then turned my cell phone off, knowing that I would be getting about eight calls within the hour.

Susan and I went to dinner and a movie and had a really nice evening. That night, I had four messages on my phone from my colleagues saying, "Whoo-hoo," "Way to go," "You are the man," and "I wish I had the guts to do that." I had a fifth message from Steve saying Brad wanted to see us in the morning.

Steve gave me a heads-up of what was to come. His advice was to just stay cool and let Brad have his say. Apparently, Brad was angry and felt that I showed disrespect to him by leaving. Not a surprise. I expected it.

We had the meeting. Brad had his say. I didn't take Steve's good advice. I lost my cool. Brad's criticism about my leaving became excessive and personal, and I said so. He didn't like my response and became angry. I responded in kind. He told me I needed to learn some damn respect, and I told him he needed to learn how to run a damn meeting. Finally, Steve stepped in and helped calm things down. And, it was over. I survived it, but it was ugly. Steve probably saved my hide.

Chapter 13

Courageous Conversations

If you are tired of office friction, a lack of candor, a failure of teamwork, toxic disputes, and pointless conflicts, you are probably more than ready to learn courageous communication.

Gus Lee

My next session with Coach Kay was a few days after my run-in with Brad. I recounted to her about my leaving a bad meeting one day and ending in a worse one the next. I gave her the details of the blow-up with Brad.

"Denny, I admire your courage for making the decision to honor your commitment to Susan, knowing that it might cause you a problem at work."

"If it comes down to it, I'd rather be fired by Brad than by Susan." I was probably sounding like I had a little more bravado than I was feeling.

"Now that a few days have passed, how is it with Brad?"

"We've only passed in the halls since then, and they weren't friendly passings."

"What would you like to see happen?" Kay quizzed.

"I'd like to restore my relationship with him, but I'd also like to talk again about our meetings. As I've thought about it some more, I feel strongly that we need to take that subject on. Our meetings are bad, and it sucks the life out of everyone, but nobody has had the courage to say so."

"What are you thinking?"

"Well, I'm not sure. Someone needs to talk with Brad and give him the feedback that everyone wants him to hear. I'm just not sure if it should be me at this point. He might hear it better from someone else."

"What does Steve think?"

"Steve agrees that the subject needs to be addressed. But he doesn't want to take on this confrontation, and no one else will touch it with a ten-foot pole right now. Everyone knows I was taken out behind the woodshed the other day. So, I think it's me or nobody. And, right now, I am willing to take the risk. I'm just not sure how to go about it."

"What I hear is that you want to try to restore the relationship with Brad and at the same time talk with him about improving the meetings. Is that right?" Kay asked.

"Right. Are those two goals mutually exclusive?" I was thinking they seemed pretty incompatible.

"Not at all, Denny. In fact, one of the skills we have to master to have relationships that work is to be able to confront people in a way that is respectful, takes on the issue at hand, and maintains or enhances the relationship. I call those 'courageous conversations.'"

"I think I did the courageous part well. It was the conversation part that didn't work?" It seemed like a tall order to me.

"It takes courage and *skills*. You've demonstrated the courage. I'll help you with the skills, if you'd like."

"I'd like."

"OK. I am e-mailing you a model I use. Let me know when you have it, and we'll go through it."

"Receiving it now," I reported back.

The Courageous Conversation Model
Adapted from *Fierce Conversations,* by Susan Scott

This model allows us to confront tough issues with courage, compassion, and skill. Learning is provoked and relationships are enhanced.

Opening statement: Write your opening statement and practice saying it out loud, in sixty seconds or less. Your opening statement should:

1. Name the issue.

2. Select a specific example that illustrates the behavior or situation you want to change.

3. Describe your emotions about the issue.

4. Clarify what is at stake.

5. Identify your contribution to the problem.

6. Indicate your wish to solve the problem.

7. Invite the other person to respond.

Interaction:

8. Inquire into their views. Listen to understand, not defend.

Resolution:

9. What have we learned? Where are we now? Has anything been left unsaid. How can we move forward?

10. Make an agreement and how you will hold each other responsible for keeping it. Thank them for their work and commitment.

Kay reviewed the model with me and then asked me to prepare my opening statement. Because this was a high-stakes conversation, she asked me to set up a call with Steve and me, so I could practice the conversation with Steve, and she would give me feedback. We did the practice session on the phone, and it was an important dry run. She and Steve gave me valuable feedback. Steve offered to go see Brad with me, but I declined. I felt like I needed to do this on my own. I made the appointment with Brad's assistant and practiced one more time at home with

Susan. Susan was extremely surprised and just as proud that I honored my commitment to her in spite of possible consequences.

I walked in with a sense of calm that surprised me.

"Good morning, Brad. Thanks for seeing me."

"Morning." Not much to tip off how Brad's mood was toward me.

"Brad, I wanted to talk about a couple of things with you. First, was to apologize for my behavior in your office a few days ago. I was defensive and angry and said some things I shouldn't have. So, please accept my apology." I started to say more but decided to stop and get a reaction.

"You were out of line." There was no acknowledgement on Brad's part that he had some responsibility in the matter, but I wasn't looking for any.

"I was. It won't happen again." I hoped I could keep that promise.

"Good. What else?" He was strictly business.

My heart skipped. The apology would be easier than the next conversation.

"The other thing I wanted to talk about is what started all of this." I took a breath. *Come on, Denny, you practiced this opening statement. Deliver it.*

"Brad, the difficulty I am having is that we spend too much time in unproductive meetings. They are often unplanned, mess up our schedules, and usually take too long. When they are planned, we have an established start and stop time, but often start late and usually go over—often way over."

I plowed ahead. "It is really frustrating to me because I am already time-pressed to run my business and can't afford wasted time. It is also affecting my personal life when the meetings run late and prevent me from meeting commitments with kids' events and with my wife.

My sense is that it is a problem that goes beyond me. I believe it is affecting the entire leadership team, and I feel a responsibility to go to bat for the team."

I continued, "I also feel a responsibility for the problem. We are all leaders in the room, and it should be everyone's responsibility to make these meetings work, not just yours. I don't think we've stepped up and done our part. I know I haven't."

I paused, looking for some reaction, and got none. "So, I am here to offer my help so that we can have more effective and shorter leadership meetings, and then get back to our other priorities."

My mouth was dry. I delivered it as well as I hoped to. *Come on Denny, keep your brain working and invite him to respond.* "What do you think, Brad?" I asked.

Brad looked at me for what seemed an eternity. His face was expressionless. I sat there thinking he must be a good poker player.

Finally, he responded. "Our meetings could be better. Sometimes, they frustrate me too." It was a grudging response. "What do you recommend?" It was more of a challenge than a question.

"I was thinking we might engage the team in how to have more effective meetings. I thought it might produce some good ideas and more ownership in it if we asked for everyone's input." After being in the field with my Kansas City team, I was starting to see the value of engaging people to produce solutions and buy-in.

"How do you propose we do that?" Brad was warming a little.

"Steve is a great facilitator of that kind of dialogue. I am sure he would be game for leading a brainstorming session." I had already talked with Steve. We both felt that Brad would be more agreeable to Steve, for a lot of reasons, not the least of which was he may still be teed off at me.

After we talked a while longer, Brad agreed to talk with Steve about it. We didn't hug or anything as a result of the meeting, but I walked out feeling like I had confronted the problem, and somewhat enhanced the relationship. At least I didn't hurt it.

A couple of weeks later, Steve led a really good meeting on improving the meetings. He received and offered some great ideas.

The team bought into taking ownership of keeping them productive and on track. Steve published what we agreed to and what we would hold each other accountable for.

Steve labeled them "The Leadership Meeting Top 10," in David Letterman fashion.

1. Schedule meetings in advance and publish an agenda.
2. Give everyone the opportunity to put items on the agenda.
3. Start and finish on time.
4. No sidebar conversations.
5. Stay on topic.
6. Debate issues with respect and candor.
7. Put it all on the table. Don't save it for the water cooler.
8. Listen to understand each other.
9. Turn cell phones off. Limit taking calls to emergencies.
10. Don't beat issues to death. Debate, decide, and move on.

About a month later, we were in one of the meetings and came to the end of the allotted time. There was still one agenda item that we had yet not covered. It was the new bonus plan for store managers. I placed it on the agenda and thought it was important because it could impact the performance of the stores. Brad started to wrap up the meeting by asking, "Are there any other items for the good of the cause?"

I jumped in. "Brad, we haven't discussed the last item, and I think it's really important that we do. It impacts the stores."

"Denny, I completely agree. It's so important; it seems to me that we need to give it the time it deserves. We are out of time now, and I want to honor the team's commitment to ending on time. I have a date with my daughter. Would you be OK with making this the first item in our next meeting?" He smiled a rueful smile as he stood up, knowing what my answer would be. While I was frustrated about not taking on my agenda item, I knew it was the right thing to do.

As we were walking out, Steve said, "Way to go buddy. You just took one for the team, and we're better for it."

Chapter 14

Leading with Values

The currency of leadership is trust.

United States Senator Chuck Hagel

By midsummer, the region was starting to push for the top spot in the company. We were building momentum. However, there was one district that was causing me concern. Jim Rogers, the district manager, was the one whose style concerned me. He is very aggressive and completely bottom line-oriented. In fact, he consistently produces bottom-line results. His style often rubs people the wrong way, and the turnover in his district is always higher than the rest of the region and one of the highest in the company.

In my second visit to his district this year, I worked with him on using more of a coaching style with his managers. He seemed to make the effort, but when he tried to get the managers to identify their challenges and offer their thoughts about solutions, they simply wouldn't open up.

It was the same way when we had the group meeting with the managers. He tried to facilitate dialogue and get their input, but they held back. It was hard to watch. After I left the district and went back home, it was really weighing on me. I decided to call a couple of the store managers whom I've known for a long time and ask them about their perspective of the week. The feedback I received that was loud and clear boiled down to these things:

- It was weird. We're not used to Jim asking us for our feedback.
- We don't speak up because we've learned. He either puts our ideas down or takes credit for the ones he likes.
- He only cares about performance and how it makes him look.
- He doesn't care about people.
- Please, don't let him know we've talked. He'll retaliate.
- He puts his best foot forward when you are in the district. When you're not, it's always his way or no way.
- We don't trust him.

A couple of days later, I had my monthly status meeting with my boss, Steve. I briefed him on the visit and my conversations with the managers.

"I'm not sure how he does it, but he is consistently one of the best performing districts in the company," was my concluding comment to Steve.

"Is financial performance enough?" Steve asked pointedly.

Silence.

"No. How we treat people matters. I guess I've rationalized his style because of his performance." No sense defending my actions.

"Have you looked at the cost of his management style?"

"Yeah, I know turnover is costing us, but I haven't put a number to it."

"So, put a number to it. What does it cost you to replace a good store manager?"

"It's hard to pinpoint. But I do know it takes about two years for a new manager to be completely up to speed. It takes time and money to recruit and interview. We invest training dollars. There is usually a downturn in store performance until the manager gets up to speed."

"So, give it a number."

"Maybe a hundred thousand to replace a good manager."

"How many good managers has that district lost under Jim's leadership?"

"Five in two years." I knew what the next question would be so I answered it in advance. "Half a million dollars, give or take." I choked the number out.

"You said his people don't trust him. What are the other costs of that lack of trust?" Steve kept pushing.

I had to think about that one. Steve waited. "Not much innovation coming out of that district. Probably because people are afraid to take the risk of trying stuff. He'll beat them down for any failures."

"What else?" Steve kept nudging.

"That district is slow to implement new programs. New programs mean doing things differently, and I think it goes back to the fear thing. They don't trust that Jim will support them through the change process. We end up spending more training dollars in that district to get them up to speed."

"What else?"

"Well, I have to spend more time on issues in his district—getting involved with people problems, interviewing new store managers. Stuff like that."

"So, what's your best guess at the total cost of Jim's management style?"

Darn his persistence. "Probably seven figures in actual costs and lost revenues."

"So, why are his numbers so good?" It was a question I think Steve knew the answer to.

"Probably because he is in a sweet market with little competition. It's pretty much cherry picking. And, because we have a core of great people who are motivated."

"Because of the district manager or in spite of him?"

"In spite of …" I mumbled.

"What could the performance of that district be with the right kind of leadership?" Steve asked.

"Huge. Best in the company."

"So, can you afford this guy?"

"No."

"Setting aside the numbers, what is our obligation to the people of that district?"

"OK. I got it. Clearly we owe it to them, I owe it to them to give them the right kind of leadership that treats them with respect and provides them with the support they need to succeed and grow."

"Great. Denny, we don't have a set of values in writing for the company. We really should, but I've developed a simple set of values that have served me well." There were four values in the set.

1. Serve the customer exceedingly well. They can buy products anywhere.
2. Treat our people like we want them to treat our customers.
3. Profit comes from doing the first two.
4. When faced with a tough decision, do the right thing.

Walking out of Steve's office, I realized I had been coached masterfully.

For the next two weeks, I worked on a succession plan for that district. A week later, I flew there and terminated Jim's employment. I realized no amount of coaching or counseling would make a difference. As a leader, his values and methods of doing business were not acceptable. I treated Jim with respect in the meeting and gave him a fair severance package. It was a difficult conversation, but the right thing to do.

Chapter 15

Breakthrough

For things to change, we must change. That is one of life's fundamentals.

Jim Rohn

It was a spectacular September evening. My favorite time of year.

It was date night with my wife, which Susan and I had kept faithfully since instituting it several months ago. I was waiting for her at the Boat House, a favorite restaurant of ours. It is in historic Forest Park in St. Louis. It sits next to a lake and is downhill from the beautiful St. Louis Art Museum. This setting is right in the middle of where the famous 1904 World's Fair was held, where hot dogs and ice cream were introduced to the world, and where Thomas Edison first displayed lighting on a mass scale. It is a marvelous setting, and we love dining outdoors.

I got there early and was reflecting on the past several months. Earlier today, I had my final coaching session with Kay, and we reviewed the results of the follow-up 360 feedback she had administered. The areas I focused on developing indicated significant growth. It seemed to spill over into other areas that were not among my micro-initiatives, but Kay's feedback to me was that she often sees where growth in a couple of areas can spill over into other areas. It occurred to me that the follow-up feedback was valuable for several reasons. First, it showed me where I made progress, and after working as hard as I had, that was important. Second, it showed what I still had to work on. Leadership development isn't a six month deal; it must be ongoing. Third, it took the guess work out of what I need to do. Leadership development is hard work, and if we are working on the wrong things, it is a waste of time and money. I committed to Coach Kay to repeat the feedback process on an annual basis.

I was feeling great that what I had been doing was making an impact. Focusing on creating clarity with my team and engaging and developing my managers was beginning to pay big dividends in the performance of my region. While my region was always towards the top of the company in overall performance, we recently broke into the lead. To me, it was a real mini-lesson in business—pick the right strategy, in this case, the micro-initiatives; add execution, which I did with the help of Kay, Steve, and the weekly scorecard; and the result was improved performance and improved job satisfaction. I was grateful that I had the opportunity to work with a great boss and coach. One of my goals is to be the caliber of coach that Coach Kay was and the caliber of leader that Steve has been to me.

I felt deeply gratified about my growth as a leader. What I found myself feeling most grateful for was getting my life back. Striking balance is still a weekly challenge, but the consistency of my targeted efforts were paying off and freeing up more time. Time to spend with the fabulous woman who was now approaching.

"Hello, handsome." She started calling me that again, and I don't think it's that I'm getting better looking.

"I'll give you an hour to stop talking like that, and then I'm whispering for help." Susan still smiles at that dumb remark and I love that about her.

We had a nice dinner, listened to the band on the outdoor stage, and talked into the evening. I felt so blessed to be reconnected with this soul mate of mine.

Towards the end of the evening, there was an interlude where we said nothing. We just gazed into each others' eyes, and I started welling up because of the way she was looking at me—again.

As Susan's favorite old sweatshirt says, "Life is Good."

Chapter 16

Developing Leaders

Some leaders want to make followers. I want to make leaders.
Not only do I want to make leaders, I want to make leaders of
leaders. Once you follow that pattern, there is almost no limit
to the growth of your organization.

John Maxwell

One year later …

I was sitting at Starbucks, waiting for my group and reflecting back on our second get-together several months ago.

After I concluded the coaching process several months earlier with Coach Kay, I felt a void. I came to realize that the value of feedback and dialogue with quality people who understand the challenges of leadership was tremendous. I felt the need to fill that void, and an idea occurred to me one day as I stopped off at Starbucks on my way to work. I saw some business people sitting at a table looking like they were enjoying each others' company while talking business. When I got to work, I sent an e-mail to Ginny Berkman, Bruce Pella, Harry Rose, and Bob Emerson. They were the people in my feed-forward session many months earlier who had given me such great input about managing my time more effectively. My e-mail was an invitation to be part of a "five-some" that would meet monthly at Starbucks to discuss leadership challenges and life challenges and enjoy each others' camaraderie. I was delighted that the response was unanimously positive.

In our first get-together, we agreed that we would meet for one hour on the last Friday of each month, and whoever could make it would be good enough. We wouldn't get hung up on perfect attendance—as long as at least three people were present, there would be great dialogue.

We would keep it informal, but if someone did have a specific issue to discuss, they would e-mail it in advance.

I was sure that having dialogue with other leaders once a month could be nothing but a positive. What I didn't know was that I would be impacted so quickly. In our second get-together, Bob asked me to review the Diamond Leadership Model I learned from Coach Kay and how I had put it to use. After reviewing the model, I said, "I keep the model on my desk as a reminder of what great leaders do. I am convinced it has helped me be a better leader and have more committed followers."

Ginny responded, "Is that what you want, followers?"

I looked at her dumbly, not really getting her question. "What do you mean?"

"It seems to me that you want other leaders in your organization, not followers."

"True," I said tentatively.

She pressed ahead. "As I understand your role, you are a regional manager and have several district managers and a bunch of store managers. Is that right?"

"Yes. I have six district managers and forty store managers."

"Then, it seems to me that while you've made tremendous strides in developing your own leadership skills, you're only scratching the surface in leveraging this leadership model. Wouldn't it be much more powerful if you focused on developing forty-six of those Diamond Leaders?" Ginny's direct manner usually hits the target.

Bruce chimed in. "What Ginny says makes good sense. It seems like a logical next step. Now that you've worked hard learning and mastering the Diamond approach, teaching it to your managers could have a lot of benefits. Common language. Common leadership principles. It could be a catalyst to building a strong leadership culture in your region. It could be a big competitive advantage."

I was fighting off getting defensive. Of course it made sense. I had thought about it and actually made a point of teaching the coaching model I learned from Coach Kay to my managers. As far as teaching the leadership model and making it part of how we lead and manage as a region, I hadn't gone that far.

"Makes sense," I responded. "Sounds like an overwhelming job. It's not like I have a huge budget."

Harry chimed in. "Maybe it won't take a big budget. Let's brainstorm some ideas for a few minutes. It sounds like the objective is to develop an entire team of what you call Diamond Leaders. Is that right?"

I nodded in the affirmative.

We brainstormed for about fifteen minutes. It was amazing. I didn't have Post-It notes handy, so I wrote down all the ideas. Later that week, I put the ideas through the idea evaluation tool to evaluate the impact of the ideas as well as the do-ability factor. It occurred to me that building a culture would take time and that my first steps were important. I decided to start with my district managers the first year, and then take it to the store managers the next year. I felt strongly that we needed to model it for the store managers first. So, what I chose to do in year one was as follows:

1. I would teach the Diamond Leadership Model at an off-site retreat with my district managers and share my own experiences with it.

2. I would invest in the 360 feedback process for the district managers and three months of coaching with Coach Kay. I would make the decision to make available an additional three months on an individual basis.

3. The district managers would review one facet of the Diamond Model in each of our meetings.

4. I would hold them accountable for achieving their business objectives *and* leading according to these principles

5. I would hold myself accountable for leading by example.

I felt strongly that these initiatives were achievable, affordable, and important, and would lay the groundwork to take it to the store managers in year two.

I was jolted back into the present moment when Bob arrived at Starbucks and whacked me on the shoulder. We were gathering for a monthly get-together. We had been at it for eight months, and the time together had been rich. The rest of the five-some arrived shortly after Bob. After exchanging the usual pleasantries and friendly kidding, Harry shared with the group that he was thinking about another job opportunity and wanted to bounce his thinking off of us. The conversation followed the pattern that had emerged over the eight months: respectful, thoughtful, candid, and meaningful dialogue, with some humor and irreverence mixed in. Harry thanked us for our thoughts and indicated that it affirmed some of his thinking, and that it added a perspective he hadn't considered. Exactly what meaningful dialogue should do!

We had about fifteen minutes left, and Bob asked me how it was going with developing my district managers. Asking me that question was like turning on a fire hose. For the next several minutes, I enthusiastically rattled off the good things that were happening as a result of developing my district managers using the Diamond Model.

- Teaching them the model did, in fact, as Bruce said it would, give us a common language and common set of values in which to lead.

- As a leadership team, we began to have more courageous conversations with each other, which led to improved clarity, better decisions, and deeper trust.

- The 360 feedback process combined with coaching from Coach Kay helped each of them understand their own strengths and identify their own micro-initiatives to make improvements in their leadership. Each of them agreed to allow Coach Kay to share the results of their feedback with me, which helped me be supportive of their micro-initiatives.

- I watched each of them begin to more fully engage their store managers in planning and decision making and could see the sense of ownership grow at the store level.

- One of the district managers made the observation that improved clarity in her district was causing her to spend less time cleaning up problems resulting from poor communication and confusion. Another added he was spending less time on *CYA* activities because of the increased trust among our leadership team. We all concurred with both observations.

- The performance of the region was steadily growing. We've held the top spot in the company two quarters in a row.

"You know," I said as I was wrapping up, "as excited as I am about where we are, I think the best is yet to come. I really believe that the most important level of management is the one that takes care of the customer. In my business, that's the store manager. When we take this Diamond Model to their level, I believe the growth of our region is unlimited."

Bob asked, "What's the biggest learning for you in this process?" It was a great question.

I thought for a few seconds. "The biggest learning for me so far is that leadership development has to be elevated to the level of strategic initiatives—the same as marketing, product development, capital investments, and other high-level objectives. As a regional manager, the thing that I can impact the most in my business is developing leaders, and so far, the results are proving that to be true. And, I find that I am having fun again."

Afterword

Becoming a Diamond
Quality Leader

I'd like to switch gears from Denny Collins' story to applying the Diamond Leadership Model to your leadership. The research behind the model that Coach Kay described in Chapter 5 was actually the author's research. I hosted a weekly radio show called *Lessons in Leadership* and interviewed scores of high-level leaders over a two year time period. I asked every guest the question Kay talked about, "What in your experience have you seen that differentiates great leaders from good ones?" That is where I came up with the Diamond Leadership Model. From that model, I've created the Diamond Leadership Workshop, which includes an upfront multi-rater feedback survey, a two-day workshop, follow-up executive coaching, and another survey several months down the line to measure improvement and identify future initiatives. Much of what is contained in the story comes from those experiences. I highly recommend the workshop for middle to senior managers.

Next, I'll take you through the six differentiators, why they matter, and questions to consider for application purposes. These are some of the exercises we take people through in the Diamond Leadership Workshop.

Differentiator #1—*Create Clarity*

One executive said, "If I could have everyone in my organization rowing the boat in the same direction, I could dominate my industry, or any industry for that matter." It is the leader's job to create clarity.

One of my radio show guests was Greg Reid, chief marketing officer for YRC Worldwide, a ten-billion-dollar transportation company. Greg shared with me that "the corporate transformation that led to the creation of YRC Worldwide began back in the late 1990s, with Yellow Corporation. Yellow and its subsidiaries needed a clear focus, a core purpose that would help guide day-to-day actions. The inspirational statement we developed then—making global commerce work by connecting people, places, and information—remains our core purpose today.

"We also listened to what our customers wanted for each business shipment:

1. Pick it up on time.
2. Deliver it on time.
3. Don't break it.
4. Bill it accurately.
5. When there's a problem, recover immediately.

"By developing and enhancing services to exceed those expectations, Yellow took the first steps on the path that led to the creation of YRC Worldwide, repeatedly listed as the most respected company in the industry by *Fortune* magazine." This is a great example of the power of clarity.

One of the things I ask workshop participants is, "As leaders, what do people in your organization or department need to be clear about?" Following is what is reported back most consistently.

- What is the purpose of the organization?
- What is the direction of the organization?
- What is changing and why?
- Who are we serving?
- What are the values that guide me when I have to make decisions?
- What am I being held accountable for?

- Specifically, what are my responsibilities, and how does that fit into the big picture?
- How am I doing?

Application Exercise

One of the individual exercises we do in the workshop is the following, which I encourage you to do.

Questions to consider: What 3–5 things would you like your team members to be crystal clear about?

1.

2.

3.

4.

5.

What is the impact of that kind of clarity?

What is the impact of not having clarity around those 3–5 items?

Differentiator #2—*Build Trust*

I asked one of my radio show guests, "What does it take to be a leader?" He said "followers." I laughed and asked a follow-up question, "OK, what is it that leaders must have to have followers?" Another one-word answer: Trust. I love it when people have the ability to boil truths down to their simple essence.

In Stephen M. R. Covey's book, *The Speed of Trust,* he makes a case that trust in an organization impacts speed and cost, two very real deliverables in today's hypercompetitive business climate.

Recently, the airline Jet Blue went through a debacle where weather problems overwhelmed them, and their systems completely broke down for several days. Hundreds of flights were cancelled, passengers experienced delays up to two days, and on some flights, passengers sat in Jet Blue airplanes on a tarmac for up to ten hours and could not get off. People were understandably furious. To their credit, Jet Blue reacted quickly with a Passenger Bill of Rights. They have also offered to compensate passengers who were treated badly during this meltdown, as well as created a payback plan for future incidents of excessive delay. Jet Blue violated the trust of their customers. According to their CEO, David Neeleman, the initial price tag of making it right is in the thirty million dollar range. It will likely take a couple of years to know the total cost.

Application Exercise

How does the presence *or* lack of trust in your organization impact speed (of getting things done, implementing change, and going to market)?

How does the presence *or* lack of trust in your organization impact costs?

Differentiator #3—*Work with Passion*

Robin Sheldon is the president of Soft Surroundings and was a guest on my radio show. She started a women's apparel catalogue business from scratch in the mid-1990s and built it into a hundred million dollar business in ten years. The company has opened its first store in St. Louis and has a second one in the works, with plans to grow a retail chain.

Going from nothing to one hundred million in ten years is amazing, particularly in the competitive world of apparel. When I asked Robin the secret of their success she said, "Passion." In fact, she went on to tell me that a big part of her success is that she hires for passion, not experience. She can teach the business to people, but she can't teach passion.

Robin Sheldon understands that a passion for the work itself is the first and biggest reward, and from that passion, business results are amplified. It is not the other way around. Great leaders have a passion for what they do, and it is contagious. You can't legislate it or fake it—you can only lead with it and hire it. Results follow.

Application Exercise

Take This Job and Love It

What deeper meaning can you find in the work you do?

What nuisances that are out of your control can you let go of?

What can you do to create a more fun environment?

What things can you do to avoid burnout (and destroy passion)?

Differentiator #4—*Serve Others*

This is the one that I believe defines the difference between a boss and a leader. Bosses expect to be served. Leaders serve. They get it that it's not about them. Bosses *may* obtain compliance from people, leaders earn loyalty and commitment. Big difference!

One of the most fascinating examples I've seen of servant leadership was with Doug Burris, Chief United States Probation Officer for the Eastern District of Missouri. When Doug took the position in the year 2000, the performance of his unit was dismal by his own admission. In fact, his belief was the whole system was broken. Doug's office supervises over eighteen hundred men and women on federal probation. When he took over the Eastern District, key metrics for his supervised population were as follows:

1. Recidivism = Not tracked
2. Unemployment = 12.1 percent (or three times the general population)

Clearly, what they were doing wasn't working. So, Doug took a different approach. He changed the mindset of his office from one of processing and monitoring people to one of getting to know them, working with them in the field, and supporting them. With that mindset change, he focused on helping them gain employment as the first priority. Although Doug was told an employment program wouldn't work with this population, he knew that the number one predictor of success was steady employment. Some 80 percent of people who are re-incarcerated are unemployed. So, Doug and his team went to work "helping" people get and maintain jobs. The results have been remarkable.

In 2006, the same metrics for the Eastern District of Missouri were:

1. Recidivism = 70 percent lower than federal average
2. Unemployment= 2.9 percent lower than the general population

Doug has received several awards for his innovation and leadership. He humbly credits his team. Their shift from policing to serving has made a dramatic difference in the lives of the men and women they supervise. They have also impacted the families of those individuals for the better and are saving taxpayers millions of dollars. Doug, like Robin Sheldon, has great passion for his work. He left a high-paying corporate job in health care to do this work because, as he told one of his children, "I love turning bad guys into good guys."

> **Factoid:** In 2006 the cost of incarcerating one individual in the federal prison system was $23,439.92 annually.

An exercise we use in our workshops is to get clear about behaviors bosses engage in, the impact from that approach, the behaviors servant leaders engage in, and the impact from that approach.

Application Exercise

In the left column, list behaviors bosses engage in, and in the right column, the impact on people and performance for those behaviors. Then repeat the exercise for leaders.

"Boss as Leader" Paradigm	
"Boss" behaviors/actions	Impact on people and performance

```
┌─────────────────────────────────────────────────────────────┐
│               "Servant as Leader" Paradigm                   │
│                                                              │
│  "Servant" behaviors/actions    Impact on people and performance │
│                                                              │
│                                                              │
│                                                              │
│                                                              │
│                                                              │
│                                                              │
│                                                              │
│                                                              │
│                                                              │
└─────────────────────────────────────────────────────────────┘
```

One of the things that come up consistently in that exercise is that servant leaders are coaches and the impact is developing people and improving performance. Mastering coaching skills may be the most critical skill for you to develop. In the workshop, we use a coaching model that helps participants develop their people. It is the one used in Chapter 10.

Differentiator #5—*Fully Engage Others*

If I could bottom-line the findings from the research that led to the writing of *First, Break All the Rules—What the World's Greatest Managers Do Differently* by Buckingham and Coffman, it is this: the best managers and organizations engage people more effectively than others, and they consistently outperform the competition. My experience is that the best leaders and managers engage the whole person, specifically three dimensions of the person:

- **Talent**—place people where their natural talents lie and help them fully develop those talents.
- **Mind**—regularly seek input and ideas from people and leverage the brainpower of the whole organization.

- **Heart**—make it a habit to recognize and celebrate the achievements of individuals and teams.

Maxine Clark has been a guest on my radio show a couple of times. Maxine is founder and Chief Executive Bear of a retail chain called Build-a-Bear Workshop. Maxine is also the author of *Building a Business with Heart*. Maxine loves being in the Build-a-Bear Workshop retail stores and hanging out with the associates and her customers. Her product, she tells me, is an experience. What I found most fascinating about Maxine is that she told me her number one job as the CEO is to listen to her associates and her customers. She indicated that many new products and operational improvements have come from her associates and customers. Maxine engages people through listening. And, not surprisingly, her staff tells me she has incredible passion for the business.

One of the questions I ask participants in the workshop is this: When people feel valued, trusted, respected, and appreciated, what is the result? The opposite question applies, as well: When people don't feel valued, trusted, respected, and appreciated, what is the result? Engaging talent, heart, and mind comes from having a deep respect for what people are capable of. Maxine Clark has a deep respect for her people and her customers. The growth of her business would suggest that it's mutual.

Application Exercise

Consider each of your direct reports. Answer these questions for each.

1. What are their natural talents? Are they being tapped into fully?

2. To what aspects or challenges of the business could they contribute valuable input and ideas?

3. What types of recognition are they most responsive to?

Differentiator #6—*Act with Courage*

I love this quote from radio-show guest Gus Lee, author of *Courage, the Backbone of Leadership.*

> Principled leaders solve moral problems. They have the courage to act rightly. They consistently demonstrate principled conduct under pressure. This gives them the strong spine to be effective and envied leaders. Backbone is what everyone admires, everyone needs, everyone wants, and everyone follows. Courage is the single most decisive trait in a leader. This is because personal and organizational crises are as routine and predictable as midtown cabs and sirens, and a manager without courage is as useful as a rowboat in a bullfight.

Barry Elbasani is executive director of a nonprofit organization called Focus on Independence. Before co-founding the organization, Barry was injured in a shallow-water diving accident. He suffered a spinal cord injury and became quadriplegic. During his rehabilitation at Craig Hospital in Colorado, Barry found himself passing his free time by going from room to room to encourage other patients. In do so, Barry found his purpose—to help and encourage others who have experienced life-changing traumatic injuries.

After returning home, Barry quickly discovered a simple task he couldn't perform became a major barrier to daily life. He wore glasses, and when they fell off, he couldn't put them back on. And, he couldn't see. The contact lens route didn't work well either. Barry's father had to put the contact lenses in and take them out. Barry laughed as he told me, "The daily trial of my father jabbing me in both eyes twice a day didn't work too well." Barry's father read an article about a doctor who performed pro bono lasik surgery for people with high-level spinal cord injuries. Barry had the surgery performed by Dr. Daniel Durrie. As a result of that experience, Barry realized what an incredible help it was to daily life to be able to see independent of daily help.

After many conversations, Barry and Dr. Durrie launched Focus on Independence. Their mission is to increase the independence of people with spinal cord injuries by reducing their need for glasses and contact lenses through vision correction surgery. Focus on Independence works to match volunteer surgeons with patients all over the country. Barry has little business and leadership training, and Focus on Independence is operating on a shoestring budget. What he does have is the passion to serve people and the courage to turn his own personal tragedy into making a difference. The Web site for Focus on Independence is www.focusonindependence.org.

Courage is a choice. Great leaders make the hard choices others won't. They confront problems, make the tough decisions, and do the right thing instead of the expedient, popular, or easy thing. They confront poor performers and bad behavior. They respectfully challenge their own leaders when necessary. They take the risks to try new things and to innovate. They turn adversity into opportunity. They are the difference makers in organizations, communities, and the world.

Application Exercise

Three Acts of Courage—Questions to Consider

1. **Be decisive.** What decisions are you avoiding that you should be making? Why are you holding back? What is the cost of not deciding?

2. **Confront reality.** What are you pretending not to know? What reality needs challenging?

3. **Tackle your toughest challenge.** What conversation am I avoiding? What is the impact of not having it?

Conclusion

I commend the Diamond Leadership Model to you as a way of thinking about great leadership, and more importantly, as a way of acting as a leader. Lead the right way, and your teams will reward you with commitment, loyalty, candor, and excellence in their performance. Then, start developing your leaders using this model, and you will begin to create a culture of greatness. Start from where you are, and do what leaders do: lead by example.

Thank you for reading *Diamond Quality Leadership*. I wish you well in your journey to becoming what this world has a great need for and a short supply of—great leaders. I hope to see you at a Diamond Leadership Workshop. For information about our leadership development programs, please visit our website at www.diamond-leadership.com, or email us a mark@diamond-leadership.com

Mark Hinderliter
St. Louis, MO

978-0-595-69356-6
0-595-69356-3